October 2006   Portland, Maine

It is with a combination of euphoria and near-disbelie~~f~~ ~~that I send this, our~~ second anthology from Moon Pie Press, out into the poetry-loving world. Since the publication of our first chapbook in 2003, Moon Pie Press has published a dizzying 25 books from 22 poets. We are so gratified by the quality of the work that has found its way to us. Our first anthology, <u>A Moxie and a Moon Pie</u>, was on Longfellow Books' list of top 50 bestsellers of 2005, and has been selected as a textbook for literature classes at both the high school and college levels. Our Moon Pie poets have excelled as well, garnering recognition, awards, and much critical acclaim—not the least of which has been the selection of eight poems by Moon Pie poets for The Writer's Almanac, hosted by Garrison Keillor.

With this, our second helping of lavish poetic delights, we have included some exotic fare "from away." Our group now includes poets from New York state, Washington state, South Dakota, Manhattan and Texas, and one part-time resident of Italy and Ireland. We're proud to include in our offerings the astonishing found poems from the papers of Thomas A. Edison, from Edison scholar Dr. Blaine McCormick. Each poet has a distinctive voice and point of view; the poems are accessible, fresh and surprising.

Give this anthology a place on your bookshelves, and you will travel with us from Belfast to Manhattan, from San Gimignano, Italy to the penguin house at the San Francisco Zoo, and to countless regions of the heart. It will be a journey you'll be glad you took.

Remember the old cereal boxes with prizes inside? They used to say in bright letters, "Collect the whole set!" Someday we'll publish Volume III, which will include selections from our forthcoming books by such fine poets as David Moreau, Karen Douglass, Ted Thomas Jr., and Robert Chute. We hope you will collect the whole set. Thank you for buying this anthology. Read carefully....there are so many prizes inside.

Nancy A. Henry and Alice N. Persons, Editors and Publishers Moon Pie Press

Note: There is a live recording CD of poets reading from this anthology, available at bookstores, from amazon.com and from our website at www.moonpiepress.com.

Full Moon Rising:
the Best of Moon Pie Press, Volume II

CONTENTS

DON MOYER (from _The Stream_)

TOM DELMORE (from _Child is Working to Capacity_)

Nymphaea

I am a painter's image
shimmering pink
afloat cloud-speckled glass
on flotilla of leaves
large as hands

my blinking light
catches the artist's eye
       brushstroke of rose flesh
       blushing to fuchsia
       crown petals ablaze
       in spotlights
       streaming through green

sky my blue mirror
transmutes azure
to indigo

though I float
tubular stems hold me
under willow's leafy sleeve

though tethered
I merge freely
with reflections of myself

rain glistened
dipped in watercolor
night folded
under stars
I am prima donna of the pond

Eva Oppenheim

On Robert Natkin's Painting
"Anticipation of the Night"

How this painted city shimmers
under lavender gauze.
Already the sky hurries
From scarlet to magenta
to opulent ultramarine.
A thousand trembling pinpricks
blink through tinted air
to no one in particular.

Lingering there on the street corner
hands in pockets
newly arrived in your windbreaker and backpack
hitchhiker, wanderer
do you sense in the immensity
of this nightly performance
the atom of yourself?

Eva Oppenheim

To My Hands

Leonardo would not have given
his Mona Lisa these hands.
No models of gentility,
you claw, scratch, clutch, hold,
conspire to reach for
what I cannot have.
Your gestures define me
when I am least myself.

Square-knuckled, broad-fingered
friends, we've hacked through
some pretty dense underbrush together,
carried baggage over rough terrain.

Transmitters of poems to paper,
melody to keys,
your touch taught me
earth, stone, water, fire,
the body's mysteries.
How often you've pulled me up
from drowning.

Strong hands have held you;
small hands have clasped you
to damp cheeks through the night.
Sometimes you comfort me
simply by holding fast
to each other.

Stiff, blue cold, swollen,
you remain haulers, lifters, pushers
even as jar covers and bottle caps
defeat you.

When other senses fade
I'll count on you to help me
feel my way in the dark.

Eva Oppenheim

Afterimage

An old man carries a child across a desert
—that is what I saw.
A woman pushes a wheelbarrow heaped with bundles
—that is what I saw.
A boy pulls a goat by a frayed rope.

I wanted to tell you how morning swings open
spills sunlight across the tabletop
on a screened summer porch
but the old man walked in front of me
carrying the sleeping child
into the desert.

I wanted to describe blue jays bickering in the maple
feng shui chimes fingering a breeze
the scuttle and scamper of woodchucks under the house
but the woman pushed her wheelbarrow across my page
her eyes the color of winter.

I wanted to show you far-off bicycles speeding silver
the pond's green croaking life
and golden puppies bounding invisibly
through waist high hay
but the boy dragged his goat into my notebook
and the rope cuts my throat.

Eva Oppenheim

The Girl in the Painting

I lost you again as soon as I found you.
Companion of my childhood, you stood
in your peaked white cap and wood clogs
on the glistening stones of that damp canal
above my bed—water buckets
yoked across your thin shoulders,
yellow braids dangling—
as the landscape dwindled and distant river boats
moaned through my sleep.
What did I know of war and dispossession?
One day I woke to your absence
in the blue room of another world where
children did not talk to paintings. So I forgot you,
did my lessons diligently, printed
loss in large letters on lined notebook paper, until
in yet another land, another room,
you reappeared in your prim white apron
not surprised to see me grown, in wavy hair
and bobby socks, greeting you in English.
Under your cool waterway,
curled on the green couch of my adolescence,
I fell in love with words, inhaled books
and wove ardent tales of unrequited love.
Eventually I left you to the care of my parents
who in turn tiptoed out of their lives
taking all trace of you with them.
So imagine my pounding heart
as I lifted a twisted bundle wrapped in old newspaper
from a closet of my mother's empty house.
Spread out on my lap
your cracked face and torn limbs
rose from the tattered tableau
of our abandoned history.
The antique dealer, schooled in resurrection,
slammed a handful of bills on the mantel,
rolled you up under his arm
and walked out the door.

Eva Oppenheim

Olga's Room

Push open the door:
Odor of camphor and wintergreen—
an old woman's overheated room.
Ointments in milk white jars
stand guard on the window sill.
A single lamp, its pleated shade askew,
casts an anemic glow.
She sits slumped at the table,
elbows on oilcloth,
head in her hands.

I jiggle my tray of steaming tea.
Chamomile mingles with unguents.
Ten years old, attracted and repelled,
locked in obedience to a family code,
I stifle in the mentholated air.

    To me she was always old,
    even those first German summers
    under the striped awning
    of our trellised balcony,
    the lace hems whispering about her swollen ankles
    where I knelt with my dolls.

I kneel to tie laces of black elephantine shoes.
Dank wool smell rises from her shawl.
My mission is to listen, not to talk.

In winter she hauled coal up steep iron steps,
married an innkeeper her stern father chose.
"But my heart," she says, touching her chest,
"my heart was with another."
The husband left, I never did learn why.
Diphtheria struck
leaving my mother her sole surviving child.

Wars punctuate her story:
Brown-shirted boys smash window panes

Eva Oppenheim

and drag old men away, while synagogues burn.
Sometimes we hobble to the armoire,
treasure-house of faded monogrammed sheets
hemmed in her once steady hand.
A knotted hand digs in between the folds
and pulls out old photographs.
(more)

       Oh how those dead children
       frightened me with their calm eyes
       staring out from the cracked brown paper
       in their neat sailor suits.

She strokes their faces;
I turn my face away.

Later, she pats my head.
I brush-kiss the parchment of her cheek
,inhaling medicated air,
then wheel around and burst across the threshold
to the embracing daylight of the hall.

Eva Oppenheim

Night

Was it the wind
that ripped me from sleep
lashing the roof
wheezing between the ribs
of the old house
where I wake feverish and afraid?

Spectral trees fling wet fingers
against window panes.
My heart explodes in a blast
of blinding light that cracks
the room in half.

I am five, in a strange bed
in a strange city
where the world tips into rage.
Thunder drives me underground
to the comfort of my own fear
inside the warmth of a down quilt
my parents dragged across continents
in our haste to escape.

Slowly the drumming rain
lures sleep, uncurls
clenched fists, weaves breath
into night rhythms, inviting
forgetfulness and the first shadow of dreams,
so when a hand suddenly touches my head
and the dark figure of my mother bends over me
I do not remember her face.

Eva Oppenheim

Things as They Are

Those trees
for instance
bending in the sun
without portent or promise
not as we translate them
into ourselves
but as they are this moment
—simply there.

This small brown spider
scuttling about its business on the sill
spinning away the hours
as they are offered
not solemn, not sad
and without bitterness
at the inevitable loss of summer.

The forest does not turn itself inside out
for our amusement.
It is merely itself
to be left alone
as it ignores us.

Yet we go on looking for ourselves
among the leaves.

Eva Oppenheim

Photographs from a Lost Childhood

In Memory of Rudy Miodownik

I do not remember why they are urging us
along the barricades.
In the photograph my coat is open and too long
and the little boy, my brother,
is crying on the shoulder of a man
whose face is turned away.

A precise shadow from the tower
fails to reach us at that angle
but I am aware of the one with the Renaissance eyes
watching me
while pretending to be easy among his roses.

Suddenly a train of sobbing
breaks through the bald hills
startling those preparing
for the procession.

The escape is scheduled
for the last minute.

I have no desire to speak in your voice
but as I begin the tones rise unmistakably
in a counterfeit of what I had imagined.
Did we invent the part about the canal,
the Commandant's beauty spot,
the steel training machines?
Why do I keep arriving at the point
where I look for myself
among the bodies?

The next picture shows a man
cradling his head in his arms.
He came from a Silesian spa
his glass still sparkling in his hand
crossing the border
like a casual Sunday stroller

Eva Oppenheim

only to find himself grieving
in a cracked landscape.

A boy in a sailor cap
holding a suitcase
stares back at the camera
from the doorway
of a shuttered house.

Where, cousin, did we lose you
along the months' dark mazes that led finally
down to a forbidden quay?

Once, when days still arrived punctually
on silver morning trays
we hoarded in our small fists
a certainty that shrank
under changing flags.

Like you, I have left shadows of myself
on old photographs
squinting into the harsh, obliterating sun.

Eva Oppenheim

Lago di Como

In memory of my mother

You smile into the sunlight
before the fountain of the Villa Carlotta
in your smart cloche, little pointed shoes,
cuffed and collared honeymoon suit,
hands on hips, head cocked
       —your trademark pose in albums of similar shots—
while the invisible bridegroom clicks his bellows camera
catching your slender figure's every turn.

It is 1930. The bridal apartment waits in a German suburb
while you inhale Italy with a great hunger
that will bring you back year after year for more than a half century
       —war the only intermission—
as bride, as widow, and later as bride again
to these sun-drenched villages, these fruit laden gardens
where I stand now wishing you could see me here.

But I was a city girl in love with the grey light of Paris winters,
the haze and clamor of spring along the Seine,
downing cups of hot tea and chocolate with existential intensity
while your postcards piled up in my room.

Oh Mutti, even then, as I resisted
the seduction of palm trees and shimmering lakes,
it was from you I was begging distance.
Your triumphs in the blazing Italian sun,
documented in Kodak color and rave reviews,
drove me deep into my film noir life
among poets of exile and gloom.

I grew up, married, had daughters of my own
who wandered off to Paris, London, Rome
while you patted my hand
and smiled over your kaffe and kuchen.

Today we meet among the cypresses
in the Villa Melzi gardens.

Eva Oppenheim

I, more than twice your age,
on the arm of my own graying groom.
Look, Mutti, across the water,
how Bellagio spreads before us
the feast of its gleaming roofs.

Water

Water

It was there at the beginning
but we were told
not to touch it was too hot
not to drink
the germs might get us
not to walk too near the edge
we might fall in.

Later we came to love the feel of wet
on our hands and faces
in the claw-footed tub
warm and soapy
or down on the beach it sneaked up on us
licked our toes with a cold tongue
and rolled out to sea again.

As grownups we gulped it
in ice-tinkling glasses
sparkling and cherry flavored
jiggling mouthfuls of cubes till
our teeth tingled.
Then we held our noses against its
chlorinated cousin in the pool.

We danced in its puddles
watered down our scotch with it
threw pennies into Italian fountains and threw
our arms up to greet great bursts of it from the sky.

Mine broke a month early.
We rushed by midnight taxi to the hospital
where water was forbidden
and when they brought you all shiny and wet
my tears watered your little face.

Eva Oppenheim

Now I lug bottles of it everywhere
take a slurp on the subway
dab wrists and brow against August heat
inhale steaming teas in dead winter.

At night it stands watch
in a tumbler by my bed.

Eva Oppenheim

Generations

On the last night of my mother's life
she spoke for the first time
on a cell phone.

It was Passover—
the sun sinking behind city roofs
spilling red light across the Seder table
set with heirloom china
silver candlesticks
the Manischewitz glowing in crystal goblets
roast lamb shank, burnt egg and parsley
nestled in their assigned places
on the painted ceramic plate.

She sat etched in light
at the head of the table
propped in her wheelchair like a queen.
Indomitable hostess
of an impeccable domain
it pained her to rule by proxy
with a slow hand.

Permitted finally
into the sanctuary of the kitchen
we trod softly and prayed
the brisket would win her approval.

I would like to believe
she looked knowingly around the circle
deep into our eyes
but actually she was tasting the charoset
I made for the first time
from her careful instructions
to see if I had got it right.

Eva Oppenheim

When my brother's cell phone chimed
and he handed it around the table
she held it like a rare conch to her ear
eyes wide in amazement to hear the voice
of a grandson in Vermont
awaiting the birth of her first great-grandchild.

With glasses raised
encircled by candlelight
in the family embrace
we did not know
death waited patiently
by her bed.

Eva Oppenheim

Spelling Lesson

When I first learned to spell my name,
I imagined that the letters had stories—
two breasts on a stick made up the P,
a tent with a crossbar made up the A,
and a headless crucifix finished off the T.

U was my favorite because it had so many stories—
it was a magnet, a jump-rope, a snake,
a falling rollercoaster, a thimble, a giant toe.
Letters were made of stories,
not the other way around.

"Spell 'color'," Sister Catherine asked.

The stories came quickly. "C-o-l-o-u-r, colour."

The cave of her mouth opened to say "no"— a perfect O,
it reminded me of a hole, a coin, a wheel, a planet.

My mother, from Belfast, had taught me to read
the children's stories she knew so that I might get ahead.
Clive and Honoria explored castles and went fox-hunting.
They had tea at four, jamcakes, holidays in the Lake District.
I read book after book about them. They were my friends.
They were good students, and they knew how to spell.

"Spell color," Sister Catherine commanded. "And this time,
spell it like an American."

"C-o-l-o...r."

          And so, I passed her class—
                    the blood in my brain
                    was purged forward.

Patrick Hicks

How to Draw a Map

My son asked me to draw a map last night.
The empty paper intimidated me,
as if I were the first cartographer.

I began like they had done years ago,
first with the seaport towns, a gathering army
that surveyed the spongy frontier of the West.
My line moved, swallowing up space—
new towns, thirsty for ink, bubbled to life and
still the border, like a black wildfire,
scorched across the translated land.

Back when the globe was British pink,
the color of skin and, by belief, civility,
native dreams were belched into the sky.
Decisions were made from
a town once called Londinium,
that garrison girdled by savages.

I looked at my son and wanted him to know
that maps are fluid and restless—
their molecules of ink, like microscopic citizens,
author the land, divert the flow of rivers, and pens.

> But I told him none of this.
> The compass was fixed. The borders solid.
> The earth would not shift beneath his feet.
> I placed an X over our home.

> "We live here. This place is ours."

Patrick Hicks

The Kiss That Saved My Life

Belfast, Northern Ireland

This never leaves me:

We came home early to drink
merlot and listen to Billie Holiday—
her voice, a secret language,
wrapped around us, and quieted
the tribal tongues of our city.

Candles shrank beneath the heavy moon,
drunks were evicted from their pubs,
and I thought about leaving your flat for my own.
I put on the armour of my trenchcoat
(it was thick, it made me look mean and tested)
but you peeled it off, you unlayered me.

We stood there,
our breath humid with wine,
and you kissed me.

Somewhere in the dark,
a drunk lit a firecracker.

                    *

Walking home the next morning,
my feet were pendulums over the paving stones—
down a sidestreet, a route I always took home,
there was something awkward, unaccountable.

My feet stopped.

The body was gone, but there was a stain—
as red as the wine that filled our glasses.
I thought about your kiss, that cracking sound,
and knew that you rescued me
from becoming another headline:
            INNOCENT MAN SHOT DEAD

Patrick Hicks

Later that night, we watched
a reporter smile from his distant newsroom.
He testified that peace was holding in Northern Ireland,
not a whisper about the other things—
    only football scores, art festivals, and happy flower shows.

Hypersensitive to the living world,
I kissed you again,
and again,
and again
and again

Patrick Hicks

Old Habits

The poison burrows
into my lungs and pollutes
my two-year abstinence.
I'm smoking again.

I have returned to Northern
Ireland, to the ease of old habits—
      the memory of blood
      the meat of human parts
      the infinite helicopters—
all are toxic,
like the ghost rising
from my lips.

Sitting in this coffeeshop,
my lungs remember
an unhealthy city.
But behind me,
the non-smoking section is
      commanded by the young,
      by their full-lunged laughter,
      and by their new stories.

Patrick Hicks

The God of War

In the humid August twilight of 2003,
Mars was closer to Earth than it had
been in 60,000 years, which might explain
why I needed some distance from you.

After a fight of some kind,
our backs were turned to each other
as we cleaned the kitchen,
dirty plates, soiled knives.

I stepped out for a smoke—
the end of my cigarette was
a ball of red, just like Mars,
hot, ready for war.

I listened to you totter about the house,
slamming this and that,
testing the landscape of our life,
while I considered the unknown space between us.

As I stood beneath Mars,
muttering my curses and platitudes,
the tiny planet lifted itself higher into the sky,
        its fierce glare dimming.

When you called my name
I stubbed out my cigarette—
confident that the red planet
would drift away, and leave us,
goddamnit, in peace.

Patrick Hicks

Nourishment

Belfast, Northern Ireland

The Rover yelped to a stop—no skitter, just two rubbermarks,
a lopsided equal sign between disagreeing poles.
The backdoor swung open and the police,
in full riot gear, jumped down to the asphalt.

I stood smoking, words choking in my mouth,
watching my Belfast breath, its smokestacks busy,
its bonfires and bunting at the ready.

As they ran into the newsagent everyone moved away, suspecting a bomb,
but I, still smoking, still transfixed, listened to the Rover's radio crackle,
as if it were underwater or sleeping in amniotic fluid—
the paint-bombs and scorches of last night tattooed onto its grey skin.

Then the police, talking of their children,
left the shop holding bags of sweets—
nourishment for the long night of riot-control ahead.

I imagined them in their armoured box,
petrol-bombs sunbursting against their cramped fortress,
eating sweets, wishing they were elsewhere.
With mouths honeyed by gobstoppers they would wait,
suck on their planets of peaceful childhood,
and concentrate on their busy tongues.

The whoosh-crack against the metallic womb of the Rover,
they would sit in the dark, waiting,
waiting, like all of us for that moment
when we are birthed into the world:
     sweets spat out, the doors explode open,
     and we see the legs of a tortured mother.

But now,
in this heavy twilight,
in this malnourished city,
I hear the Rover gear-shift up the barren street,
and watch discarded sweets-wrappers dance away.

Patrick Hicks

Shoes and Flowers

for Jon McCourt

After thirty-five years of trouble
that's what they have in common:
shoes and flowers. I've seen enough
funerals in Northern Ireland to know.

Polished shoes frame the opened earth,
flowers quiver near the fresh headstone,
the casket of another friend is lowered—
dress shoes sealed within, flowers dribbled on top.

My own dress shoes, buffed monthly,
come out when I carry caskets.
They stay in the front closet next to
my work boots, waiting.

I try to imagine a world where naked feet
are not decorated with toe tags.
They stroll instead through lush carpet,
wriggle in the sun, knead the softness.
In that world, shoes do not race bullets,
and flowers are only plucked after full-blossom.

Patrick Hicks

Lipstick Traces

When I imagine how my parents met
in a Montréal bar, on a Wednesday in 1967,
I worry that it might not have happened—
that they might have turned from each other
to unconsummate me.

Nonexistence begins when
my father walks to the restroom,
his stylish lampchops blinkering his sight,
and my mother drops something on the floor,
lipstick perhaps. They never make eye contact,
and I am blinded,
unloved.

But when I go back further,
beyond the dating of my grandparents,
and I salmon-swim through the current
of centuries, I see a school of unknown
relatives that had to love and lust,
without deviation, for me to exist as I do.

Beginning with two apes that rutted in a forest,
dead generations whisper in our blood vessels,
just like a chance meeting between my wife and me
will someday hide in the tissue of a great-
great-grandchild. Our delicate love
echoes with the shaking beds of history,
and involves more than just ourselves.

The closed door yell of orgasm
and birth, century after century,
brought my son umbilicalled into this world—
and somewhere, somewhere unknown,
a girl has been born who will look
at our boy with honeyed eyes, or—

just as likely—
she will drop her lipstick,
and never know that
he existed.

Patrick Hicks

Family Pictures

When I was a child they looked down on me,
they were fixed in oak frames, ghosts pinned
to the wall, like extinct butterflies.

The making of my father on one wall:
pioneers, they bristle with crucifixes and rifles.
I protect the distant biology of these rugged farmers,
these clerks, these railway-diggers.
The architecture of Buffalo Bill gallops
through my veins on thinned Cherokee blood.

The making of my mother on the other wall:
they pose on the family estate in Ireland.
These men in bowler hats guard beechtrees,
tennis courts, and gravel carriageways.
Their women are pressed between whalebone.
Keats wrote a poem about one of them—
an obscurity who translated Homer,
and got drunk with Shakespeare.
These Irish redcoats colonize
my faith in American history.

I am their future, their better world,
all that made them rise early,
and all that kept them working late.
When I doze before the television
I hope that I do not disappoint them,
or make them want to dissolve away,
leaving behind only tangled legacies
of prairie grass, and beechtree.

Patrick Hicks

Trying to Preserve Brian Moore's House

Clifton Street, Belfast, 1998

What remained of your childhood home
was to be smothered under the tar of a parking lot.
There wasn't much left beneath the blanket of litter,
save the chequered mosaic of your kitchen floor—
                a miserable tribute to your literary fame.

You left Northern Ireland for North America
and now I, addicted to your fiction,
reach down through the years.
I bend low and the crumbling fist-sized pieces
of your kitchen floor come to me easily.
Useful paperweights, I think. Literary history.
But the helicopters, steady as hummingbirds,
hang over this broken lot, watching.

I hear a waking bullet click—
and, still stooped, look to each corner
of your childhood garden. Nervous soldiers raise
their guns, the squawk of a radio,
my breathless chest in their crosshairs.

Time photographs itself.

Slowly, in glacial time, I pocket
your house and with surrendered hands
step away from the present.
I push through the defiant graffiti of
je maintiendrai tiocfaidh ár lá
and bring your past home,
to America.

A paperweight now, it guards your novels
and remembers how you once scooted
over its polished surface—testing your rootless legs—
waiting for that moment when you would walk away.

Patrick Hicks

Sitting on the Berlin Wall
January, 1991

On my way back to Belfast I wandered past Bebelplatz,
smelled the air for burning books, glanced at Brandenburg Tor,
and went to that open field, Potsdamer Platz.
I chewed alien words until, like the Berlin Wall,
my trust in language
collapsed.

Bordered by dead grass and foot-churned mud,
the long barrier, thick as memory, attacked the horizon,
a concrete scalpel slicing through the city.
I moved to touch it: rough, strong, as dirty as politics.

A fresh hole smashed into the Soviet concrete
allowed noisy graffiti to frame East Germany.
I clasped a hook of rebar and swung myself up
onto the back of history. I straddled the Wall,
          one foot here, the other there,
while a helicopter thumped in the distance,
its angry rotor reminding me of home, of Belfast.
I closed my eyes and hovered above that torn city—
          the puff of tear gas, the pop of bombs,
          funeral processions twisting
          through flag-ridden streets.
The so-called "Peace Line," thick as memory,
slices my ancestral city in two, cleaving hate.

Again in the middle of Potsdamer Platz,
I glanced from side to side,
and reassured the worried concrete
that there was still plenty of work to be done.

Patrick Hicks

Traveling with My Father

1. Berlin, 12 April 1995

For our first time abroad together
we decided to see Germany.
That which had been separated,
was rejoined.

We traveled the pathways of tourism,
saw this and that, bought our postcards—
you with your camera,
me with my books.

Around us, heavy cranes launched themselves
into the sky while a construction horn
consecrated the offering of metal and concrete.
The Wall was down. The world had changed.
The city was a cathedral of noise.

We searched for evidence of the Wall,
moved silently, quickly, as focused men do.
Across an open field, part of it goosestepped
lamely away from a troubled past.
We touched it together and you strolled
away, leaving me to my cigarette and
the poisonous ghosts of history.

When you called my name,
you were on the other side.
Rusted rebar framed you
and we stood there, father and son,
looking at each other through the broken wall,
understanding.

Patrick Hicks

2. *Dublin, 16 June 1997*

The sun was asleep when we rode the swaying train to Dublin.
You with your camera, me with my bruised copy of *Ulysses*.
We were going to walk literature's Mecca.
It was my idea, but you, the polymer chemist,
seemed happy to contemplate the bonds between us.

On that Bloomsday, we bought our lemon soap,
visited Martello Tower, and walked along Sandymount Strand.
I, your son, the writer, explained how Stephen Dedalus
never connected with his father. It was over

burgundy and gorgonzola sandwiches
that I showed you a map of Dublin.
I traced my finger over the wandering rocks of
missed opportunities between Joyce's characters.

When I finished speaking,
you ordered two pints of Guinness.
We drank silently, together,
until the darkness had been captured.

You licked foam from your lips,
scratched the bristle of your face,
and you sat back, smiling from the street,
to me. When we crawled back to Belfast,

our mouths were weak but our memories
were as alert as the first day
that you cradled me,
and wondered who I was.

Patrick Hicks

3. *Lake Superior, October 1999*

As we sat on the cabin porch,
the suburban cobwebbing of Minneapolis
became a memory. Pine trees supported the sky,
a pink sun dissolved into a freshwater ocean.
Board games lounged between us,
crushed beer cans slept on the floor.

"Dad?" I whispered.

No answer, you were asleep,
testing oblivion.

I felt your absence and knew that someday
you would be gone. Tell me, when your own father
traveled on ahead—his lungs bloated with mucus—
did the world seem this dark, this full of shadow?

I considered my future self
sitting next to a stranger,
one that I had raised from birth.
That child, linked to the foggy roads of your past,
might one day bleat into the gathering darkness,
as I do now:

            Dad?

Patrick Hicks

Ode to Teenagers' Hairdos in June

Today the teens' bouqueting faces
from the gazebo's railed vase
have hair shaped into flowers
whose Latin roots escape
the brain's gray matter

as this girl's blue-highlighted curls
turn her into a psychedelic tulip
and this boy's orange and black-dyed spikes
morph him into the world's tallest marigold
whose eyebrows dragonfly with delight.

It's as though they're playing out
some pagan ritual they intuit
and the purple and green roots
have nothing to do with hormones roller-
coastering the cardiovascular—

it's as though the hair
literally has a mind of its own
and will blossom its exotic beauty
despite how they might pass out
on the liferaft of their lover's mattress.

And today, with the yellow
periscopes of Russian sunflowers
a month away
and choirs of purple iris
already silenced
by June's dryness,

even the mother with retarded ten-year-old in tow
slows to marvel
at this Garden of Eden of Teens
before sitting by the river's magic carpet
where she thinks her hair, soon,

Dennis Camire

will be a strange off-gray or blue
as she still cares for the son
who'll never color his hair green
though, in his fifties, likely,
still seduce her into this world's strange beauty

the way he always blossoms
that same smile to each unexplained glory
which, maybe, she now realizes,
is the only flower any mother could desire
growing over her grave

under the iris blue sky
that, too, on our best day
often feels like the perfect hairdo
though held in place
and fine-tooth-combed by crows....

Dennis Camire

Ode to a Maine Moose

French kisser of bogs,
rainbow trout, and polliwogs—
brothel for black flies,
mosquitoes, and fleas—train derailer,
epicenter, and slow, soft gazer....
with a beard resembling that
of the turkey and the Yogi—
with the crown of a corrupt,
colonial king, the patience
of Job, the sadness
of a Modernist, the legs
of a llama, and the ears
of a deer—you are so strange
you could be
God.

Dennis Camire

Ode to Teaching Simile at a Midwestern University

I said "you need to see a feather
as a tree from the forest of pheasant."

I tried fusing the two brains with
"a watch is like a moon with a mind."

And a few went on to write:
"a purse is like money's mouth

and "a crow flying to roadkill
is like the grim reaper's directional."

But most feared simile
disguising those Magnum-Opus-emotions

in those essays about being
the only lesbian in Midland, Kansas

or desiring to fail senior history
because they hadn't a parent

to snap the photo when the diploma
was batoned into their sweating palm.

My graduate student challenge:
to convince them simile isn't like

a burkah placed over a wife's face
to mute the indignity that might

stamen from her gaze. Oh, frustrated
with their continued frustration

I felt like the soccer coach
making players follow through

on all those strange yoga poses
moments before the championship game—

I felt like the Zen master
stressing breathing

to the novice seeking
to see the Buddha in the

next lotus he walks over.
But gracefully that open-

Dennis Camire

admissions university
allowed for my own improvement

and future lessons in simile found me
vivifying things by beginning with

"the heart is like an accordion
too few of us learn to make sing

though the left and right brains press
so many buttons and squeeze

a slew of keys." And gleaming
the possibility of a simile

filleting some of their salmon-pink feelings,
one imagined "desire like

the scarlet runner bean blindly
clinging to pole and chicken wire;"

another saw "the heart
as a catcher's mit

in the fast-pitch tournament
of adult relationships."

But it's how most come to trust
how truth can be beauty

and beauty can be truth
and how one or two

secrete you poems or essays
where the exact simile releases some of the

pain of their mother's suicide
or guilt from their ninth-grade rape,

that has me saying to you:
"it's true, you do learn so much

from your students for just like
I was saying to my teacher-friend Marita:

'sometimes there's just nothing to
compare the beauty of these students to.....' "

Dennis Camire

Ode to the Letter F or "Fat-free Metaphysics"

Always arriving farm-fresh,
                    feathered, and eff-ervescent
in "affection," "fandango," and "farfetched"
                    "fff" effuses from us this
mystical, primal "force
                    that through the green fuse
drives the flower"—
                    f's flashflood of breath
freed with the meekest
                    "ffig," "ffit," and "ffolly"
setting the spirit ffree-
                    floating the body—
f's follow-through
                    in crossing the finishing lines
of tarifff, tough, and fisticufff
                    all the feedback needed
to fathom the reserve force
                    waiting to Air Force Fighter
along the disputed borders
                    of our lives....Yes, fff,
no other letter so fueling us
                    to follow our fancies
as you unfurl the flags of
                    "fruitful," "fantasy," and "fulfill"—
no other letter
                    a more effective "freedom fighter"
as a flurry of "faith,"
                    "freewill," and "reform"
infects the fallen
                    with this phoenix-
rising-out-of-the-ash-feeling
                    that they can escape
their awful Fate and move on to
                    the next phase in their life
where they "save face."
                    Any wonder, then, f,
I fixate on you to affirm
                    our alphabet can flesh-
out our metaphysical essence
                    and form phantasmagoric words
which fillet feelings
                    and fresco body and soul
with Florentine finesse?
                    Any wonder you foolproof
how "forgiveness" and "unfailing faith"
                    can be made flesh
with the mere flash

Dennis Camire

                    of a focused and affectionate tongue?
And so, fff, let all the forlorn
                    suffering "the slings and arrows
of outrageous Fortune"
                    St. Francis at the Fatima of your font
in order to floral
                    your Old Faithful-like force
when the fairly tale marriage
                    fails at forty-something
or they find themselves, at fifty,
                    still feeding the same fleece
at the factory which foiled
                    their father's youthful fancies.
And as for your own future fff,
                    the pharisees and I foresee
your folk-pharmacy of "freedom,"
                    "fortitude," and "fe fi fo fums"
Jolly-Green-Gianting
                    the feeble and fainthearted
to finally give the
                    fascist, fitful, foreman the finger
or forget their femme fatale past
                    and follow their feelings
all the way to their rainforest floodplain.
                    Yes, fff, you will be
the Sophist philosopher
                    proofing how formidable
a single soul can be if
                    looking within and knowing thyself
fully!—you will be the fission
                    fueling the prophecy
of the "meek inheriting the earth"
                    and "the house of the father!"
All that's left now ff
                    is the conscious "effort"
to fathom how no hard facts,
                    fuck-ups, or folly-happy Falstaffs
can foil your fossil-
                    fueling our dreams
into self-fulfilling prophecies
            until, accumulating so many of your frequent flier miles
and manifesting our destinies
                    at the velocity of ferocity,
we see how the final test of f,
                    in effect, is fathoming
how to ingest all this
                    formerly forbidden fruit
served up to us now
                    with the fury of fastfood.

Dennis Camire

Ode to the Letter G or "Oh Mother of God Sweet Jesus"

—for my aunt and grandmother—

With a grin and jowls
making cursive J
green with envy
G's simply gorgeous
even while grieving,
gossiping, and grandiloquently
prophecying gloom
and Armageddon
for every generation.
Yes, G's GQ visage
and garrulousness
so ingratiate
that we deem him
congenial and gentrified
even when he gratuitously
sentences the guilty
to gallows
and guillotine;
and G's gift
to get one giddy
with the giggles
and to drown a grim
and grotesque existence with
an endless supply of gravy
mutes opposition
to how he
always leads "grace"
and grandiosely claims
that he best speaks
for all that's "good,"
"God," and "glorious"
in this great, big galaxy.
And on the anniversary
of my grandmother's
death, who'd have guessed,
G, I'd envy
the way you keep
your chin up
when shipwrecked
on the island reef of "grief?"

Dennis Camire

Who'd had gambled
you'd be my guru my Gandhi
as I grapple with
a life of grace
and goodwill
not guaranteeing
a death free
of radiography
and the tumor's
gratuitous growth
after she pleaded,
"Sweet jesus,"
to just let her "go
to her grave
and God...
Yes, G, grant us
your guts and gallantry
to give the Grim Reaper
your same gritty grin
if we too don't go
so "gently into
that good night"
with a gloating profile
exclaiming how
we're going to our God
remembering all
the gifts we gave,
ingrained, in the voices
of the next generation.
And grandmother who died
before I could say anything
but "gee" and "gosh"
through eulogy
and burial, let me
finally let go
of the grief that's so
gripped me as,
at the end of your ode,
my chin shapes
into the G of saving grace
in saying: "see, now,
your grandchild's eyes
finally turning into
the two beautiful o's
of "goodbye," crying.....

Dennis Camire

Ode to the Letter V or: a Reply to Venus

All Verve, Verb, and nerVe
        wearing your tight V-neck
and re-Vealing
        a little too much cleaVage
even as you sit
        a "conVert" in the "conVent"
or deliver the man-
        slaughter Verdict,
verily I say unto V:
        "you're a bit of the vixen
and volkswagon van free-luv-spirit"—
        yes! your broad-shouldered
thin-hipped pelvis the enVy
        of the well-proportioned PeneloPe
and causing the bodacious B
        to tighten her belt around
her Buddha-esque belly.
        And every Victor, Vanessa, and Valentino I've known
always spending eVenings with lovers who
        bring Vivaldi or Vallejo to the vino and veal
on the vine-covered-veranda. Yes, "Vvveee,"
        you exude this vvvibe   which Vvvvivifies
Ivy League Virgins
        into veering into the
vortex of their inner diVa!—
        you viagra our vocabulary
until each v in "vibrato,"
        "vigor," and "vavoom"
is a saber-toothed tiger-incisor
        tearing into our sexual
and celestial desires!.
        Oh, the vertigo
of your Cuervo Gold ode
        and the Courvoisier Vsop
of "violets," "violins," and "violence!"
        Yet lately v, lacking the Cape Verdes
of a lovely Eve's body
        to alleviate this feeling

Dennis Camire

that all in life is vain,
                    I see how a beVy of lost loves caused me
to vilify this primeval Eros you Vesuvius
                    and to believe you a medeival, vulgar tongue
invoking "diva-stating" women
                    eviscerating the heart's rounded v.
Yes, v, I stared into your blackbird wings
                    and envisioned them opening the way
for a Visigoth-like invasion
                    of vices and venalties
for the most venerable of souls ....
                    Yet trying to mute the flirtatious Venus of you
when speaking to Victoria-Secret-women
                    whom I desired, secretly, to
Venus-fly-trap the body,
                    didn't free me from love's vicissitudes
or the viscous cycle of relationships where I
                    struggle to give as much as much
as I receive. And life, v—
                    cleaving too much to Victorian virtue—
soon reveals itself to be invitro
                    and loneliness inveterate for the most
veteran Casanova.....
                    And so v, the question
I now see clearly is simply:"
                    to v or not to v!"
Love's reVolution impossible
                    if not willing to decree:"live V or die!"
And so think, inVariably, v,
                    of your ode as performing
a "reVerse Vasectomy"
                    where reconverting to the reformed Veda
of your sexy voice and vision,
                    returns my virility and virtuosity
in the topsy turVy world
                    of trying, without a Virgil,
to realize the vision
                    of my own Beloved.
And yes, ViVas too V
                    for all the disheartened feeding intraVenously

Dennis Camire

off these lines until inspired again
                              to freely squeeze the
accordion of each V in conVersation
                              and serenade lovers they never conceiVed
into whirling derVishing
                              into their vicinity....until, with this reViVal
of so many souls dancing again
                              with the Shiva of V,
no more lost visions of "love
                    inspiring the heart's pink flamingo
to flap her wings in the
                              aViary of the ribcage and, maybe, v
only this everlasting praise
                              for your electrocardiogram across the page
revealing a heart still speaking
                              love's language and remaining
vulnerable to beaching their body
                              upon the Vineland or Valhalla a new lover
for loe is love, surely, without these
                              quantum string vibrations of V
and what is love, really, but the final "victory."

Dennis Camire

Ode to a Capital, Cursive J or
"My Own Personal Jesus"

Though cursive's designer
                    gowns of sound
make the formal F fashionable
                    and shapeshift the serpentine S
into a sexed salmon
                    swimming through
"sacristy" and "sweetness,"
                    cursive J's double-jointed nature
made her the crown jewel
                    when skywriting each letter
across the homework page
                    as the freedom to
"jerrymander" her borders
                    as long as legible to Sister Jackie
"and not demeaning
                    Jacob, Joseph, and Jesus"
launched your "first creative journey
                    in discovering yourself
scribing dragonfly wings
                    and the rollercoaster's
giant lollipop of a loop-de-loop .
                    And the intoxication
of engaging in
                    cursive J's jazz improvisation
until composing your own
                    poetic King James translation
revealing you had a unique beauty
                    to bring into being
and would push beyond the boundaries
                    of simply being known as the
jock, jokester, or joint-toking, jaded teen....
                    And it was cursive J's
strangly coiled DNA
                    which wiggled its tail
before bravely explaining
                    to your high school Juliet
why your "journey" had to take you
                    away from the jumper-cables
of her embrace
                    which jacuzzied every drop in
the body's Red Sea—
                    it was j's Jersey shore u cruised

Dennis Camire

before the Janis Joplin in you
                    declared to the judge
and jury of your father
                    that you were going to be
the "hip-hop DJ" instead of the
                    journeyman journalist
or internist from Johns Hopkins....
                    Yet looking through
those teen journals
                    you sometimes feel jilted
as bravely forging your own trail into
                    the jungle of this unique, creative you
is yet to manifest that job
                    which grabs you by the jugular
or that lover who, by Jove,
                    sends you into the jetstream of "jubilee."
And some of you, too, feel life
                    might just be an "infinite jest"
as the doctor discovers the tumor
                    just days after the honeymoon
or the afternoon your lover
                    dropped to his knees
and, pouring the JD
                    down the drain, promised to be more
like Jesus than Judas.
                    Oh, the Jerusalum of this midlife you
struggling to enjoy the journey!
                    The personal "jihad" needed
to stave off the feeling
                    that 'life might just be
one great big joke'
                    for God's giant "Jumbotron!"
Yet, unlike O, cursive J's
                    strange, uroborus shape
never promises your journey
                    comes round neatly full-circle
so—at the height of your jetset life—
                    you won't suddenly find yourself
nosediving
                    into a Sea of Japan
when eulogizing a wife
                    who's June to your January
or identifying your son
                    who slipped through the ice
and died with your diamond jig
                    pierced to his dropped jaw.

Dennis Camire

And cursive J's
                              "wandering Jew" nature,
anticipates your daughter, one day,
                              possibly choosing the straitjacket
over your embrace
                              and how you, too, might pray
your grandmother forgets
                              her heart medication so she's saved
from watching her eighty-eight
                                          pound jaundiced daughter
pass from her second round of radiation.
                              And so today, trying not to fishtail
on J's strange drag-speedway
                              as you find yourself "separating"
just weeks after adopting the new baby
                    or wondering how your uncle could be found
hanging in the county jail,
                              justice requires scribing J after J
until seeing, like Job,
                              how J eventually ties up all
the loose ends of her tail neatly
                              and promises closure, consolation, or compensation
for all of life's unforseen junkie to
                                          jesus freak transformations.
And now seeing with the Jungian cursive J
                              how "the end of all our exploration might be
"to arrive where we began
                              and know the place for the first time,"
how much easier to be
                              lost inside inside the belly
of Jonah's whale
                              when seeing, at forty, how
"most likely to succeed" is still
                              the "Average Joe cleaning homes
or "Plain Jane" mother of three surviving
                              a second decade without feeling
the dovetail joinery of uniting
                              with her soulmate. Yes, how much more space
the small, unbidden joys have to resonate
                              in simply solving the daily jumble
or singing, unexpectedly, with the Blue Jay
                              whose black-winged beak—opening
and closing in song—might be
                              the only "jaws of life" available
to free us into the birth and beauty
                              of each strange, new day.

Dennis Camire

Every Window

Another time we experimented
with a tub full of soapy water
and put hydrogen into it to make large bubbles.

One of the boys who was washing
bottles in the place had read in some book
that hydrogen was explosive,

so he proceeded to blow the tub up.

There was about four inches of soap
in the bottom of the tub 14 inches high,
and he filled it with soap bubbles up to the brim.

Then he took a bamboo fishpole,
put a piece of paper at the end
and touched it off.

It blew every window out of the place.

Blaine McCormick

The Fundamental Basis for a Lie

Fish seem to be rather conservative
around this bay.

One seldom catches enough
to form the fundamental basis
for a lie.

Dante left out one
of the torments
of Hades.

I could imagine a doomed mortal
made to untangle wet fish lines
forever.

Everybody lost patience
at the stupidity of the fish
in not coming forward promptly
to be murdered.

Blaine McCormick

I Hadn't the Nerve

After I had made
a great number of inventions
and obtained patents,
the General seemed anxious
that the matter should be closed up.

He called me into his office
and said,
"Now, young man,
I want to close up
the matter of your inventions,
how much do you think
you should receive?"

I had made up my mind
that taking in consideration
the time
and the killing pace I was working
that I should be entitled
to $5,000,
but could get along with $3,000,
but when the psychological moment arrived,
I hadn't the nerve to name
such a large sum,
so I said,
"Well, General, Suppose you make me an offer."

Then he said,
"How would forty thousand dollars strike you"

This caused me to come
as near fainting
as I ever got.

Blaine McCormick

Over The Wire

While learning to telegraph
I and a boy named Clancy,
built a telegraph wire between our houses,
about a mile apart,
separated by woods.

The wire
was that used for suspending stove pipes,
the insulators were small bottles
pushed on ten-penny nails
driven in the trees.

It worked fine.

My father had a neighbor named Jos. Symington,
a highly educated Scotchman,
and they would talk politics nearly every night
until I returned from town,
which varied from 11 p.m. to 1 a.m.

I would save one paper,
but many nights
when I wanted to practice
I would give the paper to Clancy
and then my father
would have to get the news
over the wire
or not get it at all.

This generally resulted in going to bed
at 3 a.m.

Blaine McCormick

To Save All I Could

One afternoon
about a week before Christmas,
our train jumped the track
near Utica.

Four old Michigan Central cars
with rotten sills
collapsed in the ditch
and all went to pieces,
distributing figs,
raisins,
dates,
and candies
all over the track and ditch.

I started in
to save all I could of this
by eating it.

Our family doctor
had the time of his life with me
in this connection.

Blaine McCormick

An Angels' Picnic

This is by far
the nicest day of the season,
neither too hot nor too cold –

it blooms
on the apex of perfection –

an Edenday.

Good day for an angels' picnic.

They could lunch
on the smell of flowers
and new mown hay, drink
the moisture of the air, and dance
to the hum of bees.

Blaine McCormick

Nicodemus

I

Just before the war broke out,
there came to the train one afternoon in Detroit,
two fine looking young men
accompanied by a colored servant.

They bought tickets
for Port Huron,
the terminal point for the train.

After leaving the Junction,
just outside of Detroit,
I brought in the evening papers.

The train was called
the accommodation and there was only
one passenger car.

When I came opposite the two young men
one said,
"Boy, what you got"

I said, "Papers"

"All right"

He took them
and threw them
out the window
and turning to the colored man said,

"Nicodemus,
pay this boy."

I told him the amount
and he opened a satchel
and paid me.

Blaine McCormick

The passengers didn't know
what to make
of this transaction.

II

I returned
with the illustrated papers
and magazines.

These were seized
and thrown out the window
and I was told
to get my money of
Nicodemus.

III

I then returned
with all the old magazines
and novels
I had not been able to sell,
thinking perhaps
this would be too much for them.

I was small
and thin
and the layer reached above my head
and all I could possibly carry.

I had prepared a list
and knew the amount
in case they bit again.

When I opened the door
all the passengers roared
with laughter.

I walked right up to the young man.

One asked what I had;

Blaine McCormick

I said, "Magazines and novels."

He promptly threw them
out the window
and Nicodemus settled.

IV

Then I came in
with cracked hickory nuts,
then pop corn balls
and finally
molasses candy.

All went out the window.

I felt like Alexander,
the Great.
I had no more chance,
I had sold all I had.

V

Finally,
I put a rope to my trunk,
which was about the size
of a carpenter's chest
and started to pull this
from the baggage car
to the passenger car.

It was almost too much for my strength
but finally I got it
in front of these men.

I pulled off my coat
shoes
and hat,
laid them on the chest,
then he asked

"what have you got boy"

Blaine McCormick

I said

"Everything sir,
that I can spare that is for sale."

The passengers fairly jumped
with laughter.

Nicodemus
paid me $27
for this last sale
and threw the whole out the door
in the rear of the car.

VI

These men were from the South
and I have already retained
a soft spot in my heart
for a Southern gentleman.

Blaine McCormick

No Reason to Doubt

If the world wags on
for many thousand years more,
there would seem to be no reason why
men should not go on
discovering and inventing.

No reason to doubt
that new tricks and arrangements will be made
so that Nature may work
to man's advantage.

The scientific journals will go on publishing,
Poggendorrff the Philosophical Mag.
will be full then as now.

It is unreasonable for men today to be afraid
that they cannot find out any more
that all has been found.

Blaine McCormick

The Percentage of Crooked People

The percentage of crooked people
was smaller when I was young.

It has been steadily rising
and has got up
to a very respectable amount now.

I hope it will never reach par.

Blaine McCormick

A Little Deaf

It's nice
to be a little deaf
when traveling.

You can ask
everybody directions,
then pump your imagination
for the answer.

It strengthens this faculty.

Blaine McCormick

The Smell of Tuberoses Will Spoil My Appetite

One night I was walking up Broadway
and went into Kohn's Museum of Anatomy,
which place I have always wished I never entered.

In this place were all kinds of bodies
and parts thereof
molded in wax,
many of them illustrating the eating away of flesh
by certain malignant diseases.

The place had many urns
filled with tuberoses,
which gave an overpowering smell.

For two days I couldn't eat a thing,
and to this day the smell of tuberoses
will spoil my appetite.

Blaine McCormick

Where the Little People Live

We do not remember.

A certain group of
our little people
do this for us.

They live in the part of the brain
which has become known as
the "fold of Broca."

Broca discovered and proved
that everything we call memory
goes on in a little strip
not much more than
a quarter of an inch long.

That is where the little people live
who keep our records for us.

Blaine McCormick

At the Yoga Studio

a mouse rummaged
through the cold night,
chewed a determined hole
in the wicker basket,
nibbled off the corners
of twenty little cushions
to get at the rice inside
and make a nest of silk.

In the morning,
the people lay
in corpse pose
savasana
with no covers
closer to the earth.

Marita O'Neill

Belly Dancer at *The Vagina Monologues*

She begins with her back to the audience—
with golden-orange lights that follow the sinews

of her body like the morning sun, defining
the curves of a landscape. Bare midriff, hips hung

with dangling silver coins, ankles covered in golden bracelets,
a black braid hangs against her spine. Her arms are lifted

like serpents above her shoulders, one leg pauses
mid-air as the music begins to whirl into images

of white sands, heat, the mystery of covered things.
It is her hips that move first, almost imperceptibly,

as if the drums were coming from inside her body.
Woman and music inseparable, her bare back

flowing with the rhythm, her arms a different being all together,
lithe, muscular, gliding with a controlled mastery.

A trill of flutes, the dervish and fever of drums
don't dim our silence filling the hall. We watch

spellbound as if we had never seen a body dance.
Then she begins to turn, a slow coax and sway

of hips to drum, her sweat and silver catching light,
and suddenly we see her belly—

not flat and rippled, but round,
                    enormous and celestial,

hanging heavy with life, a woman just days
from giving birth. And there is nothing on that stage

except the complete fullness of this instant:
her thick breasts, all the parts of her dancing,

her body light as a girl's, her radiance
so dazzling, it is hard to look; as the music stops,

she stretches her arms wide as the lights
catch them and reach out beyond her body.

Marita O'Neill

Working at the Homeless Shelter

I had never been so close to a man stripped of his skin, wings
broken like a bird frantic to escape from its own insides.

Packed that night, the shelter smelled of tired feet and sour bodies,
a moldy church basement—rows and rows of cots. All those poor

people coughing with the radiators, breathing in the red light
of the exit signs while the steel mills hissed like tombs along the river.

This winter hurts deep into the bones where I buried you in the past
that night, you appeared at the shelter door—your eyes panicked

in their own sockets. Dangerous, I assumed; limbs jerking and twitching
as you talked, your words a sweaty ramble: prison, no food, nowhere to go.

Dangerous, on the phone, my supervisor told me, *tell him he's got to leave.*
How could I send you out into three degrees below zero? Not just once,

but again after you had hidden under the stairs, curled up like a shadow,
shaking, so human. There are crimes that pass like a wind slipping out

a closing door. But eyes, eyes can't really be forgotten, so sometimes
I imagine that night differently: your hair in a violent tangle, deep-purple skin,

polyester jacket zipped to the neck. And I ask you, *So why were you in prison?*
What happened? You mumble, *It was a stolen ham and cheese.*

A lousy sandwich. I get you a blanket, pillow, apologize for the hard floor.
Tonight, my thoughts fall like snow, through which memory

makes its footprints in an empty winter street long past midnight.

Marita O'Neill

Standing on the Dead

Locking up in the morning, I never got used to the way
the people would disappear as the sun was rising
and the fog moved in along the streets.
At night, they'd be waiting in the church cemetery

for the shelter to open, or smoking on the manicured
prep school lawn beside it. They'd lean
against the tombstones talking, or curl up sleeping
under the colonial oaks. Gloria from Haiti

would wait in the church doorway,
her tall up-do wrapped in a bright scarf, telling me,
Standing on the dead's bad luck; I'm not bringing
bad luck on me, no man. She slept on a cot

in the hallway because the women's room
faced the dead; *I don't want ghosts in my dreams,*
and I didn't blame her. One evening Art showed up
with a cast on his wrist and another on his foot

after falling two stories during a painting job.
I'm a hazard to my own health, he'd laugh
through two front teeth folded crookedly together.
In that condition, one day he stole a yellow Strohman's

bread truck, baffled when he was picked up by the cops
speeding down Rt. 95 an hour later. Back from prison,
he wouldn't talk to anyone, or explain why he drove
and drove that day, except to say, *I had to get away.*

I was too young then to know why I took such comfort
in these people who were long past pretense, who couldn't
be anything but imperfect.   Seeing them each night
with their feet on the tombstones, and hearing their stories

I loved them the way you can love strangers,
for showing in their blessed irreverence
how they defy the dead, defy the cruelty of living, refusing
in their brokenness to be anything less than human.

Marita O'Neill

The Curve

Slipping a cheat-sheet underneath the left thigh
of his polyester shorts, Mark McBrady tempted the odds—
11th grade algebra, Immaculate Conception High,
final exam. Sitting in the last seat behind him,
I spent most of the exam (which I failed),
watching him un-suck his skinny thigh from the seat
and glance with a twitchy nonchalance first
at Mr. Ozzie, our jock-coach turned math general,
then at the thumb-sized paper he had scratched full
of desperate hieroglyphics. When Mr. Ozzie
cowboyed down the isle and asked Mark
to stand up, my heart sank. I could see
Mr. O's "gotcha" face fall into disbelief
when Mark stood, and the seat was empty.
Under the desk, on the floor, in Mark's pockets
they searched, turning again and again—baffled,
while that lovely sheet hung on the sweat
of Mark's thigh for three glorious minutes
full of the thrill of not getting caught, of fooling
the bad guy, winning a game that can't be won.
Until at last, Mark sat down, and that tiny bit
of magic peeled from his leg and twirled
like a surrendered flag onto Mr. Ozzie's smug shoe.

***

Racing again, late for school, and I'm playing
that game with time: drink coffee, eat
a Poptart, put on mascara & check my teeth
in the rearview—ten minutes saved.
Another yellow light, and I'm convinced
it's possible to fall into that puzzle Hawking
tells us exists in "the curve" where time
disappears into infinity; so now I'm praying
to The Curve, or maybe it's the second Fate,
the one who pulls the strings; maybe she'll grant
me the time I need.   Other have done it—
there's Uncle Jack: smoked and drank all his life,
lived to be 103, as if he wormed his way
through the holes, the folds that Hawking tells us
make the boundaries of time porous, bendable.
I pull into the high school parking lot with five minutes to spare.

Marita O'Neill

My cousin Steven, ex-priest converted
to marriage, now a Protestant-dad, has my family crying
we're laughing so hard—his kids having never seen
a cross hung with an actual "Jesus" until the day
of their grandfather's funeral. Riveted to the fleshy
Jesus hanging from the ceiling, they sat in silence,
staring up: hands and legs punctured with steel,
blood dripping down his lanky body.
Mama, what did they do to Jesus?
Are they going to do that to Daddy?
Her mother fumbles, trying to explain while
her little girl, hands gripping the pew,
yells out, *Jump, Jesus, jump!*

Growing up Catholic, we were accustomed
to the image, always reminded he
was up there for us, for *our* sins.
In the second grade, I confessed I was mean
to my hamster, and invented sins, hoping
my endless list would make it all worthwhile.
They told us he rises at the end of the story.
So is it cheating to hope now that pieces
of the story are true? That my dad at 84
will find that curve into infinity,
or that Mark McBrady is somewhere
beating the odds? I was sympathetic
with the apostle Thomas for needing
to stick his hands into Jesus' wounds
as if in the heat of the blood he could
tell the difference between hope
and the void vying for its place.

Marita O'Neill

Evidence of Light

Remembering the Frank family's last day,
Hanna Schroeder is certain of the table—
it was set for lunch. It was she who had to show them in,
walk them to the third floor, watch them destroy
the bookcase that hid the door. *No!* Eric Schuler
is emphatic, *It was not that late in the day.*
As their friend, he remembers the morning light
streaking in on the east side of the room, the dust
suspended, dancing in white circles below the window,
the table not yet set for lunch. What does this matter now
this table prepared, this evidence of light
like the shadow of a star in the night sky?

**

With the white sands of the desert, American soldiers
filled the sand bags, mistaking shattered pieces
of ancient Babylon for dirt, mixing bits of brick
and road, chips of cups and bowls with sand.
Maybe a woman 3,700 years ago washed that bowl
and handed it to her boy where on the low table
he arranged them—the saucers still glistening
with the cold waters of the Tigris, catching light.
Maybe that same day the father brought news:
a great black pillar, inscribed with cuneiform,
a code of law born to humankind—eye for an eye, tooth for a tooth.

**

We lived by a particular code
when I was young—the law of erasure:
every evening my mother and father hid
the bottles: Budweiser, cold duck, whiskey.
And every morning I'd search for them,
digging in the trash cans, behind the bushes,
underneath couch cushions. They were always
empty, and I imagined lining them up like witnesses
in a row along the kitchen table, letting the light
pass through their hollow bellies like a silent screaming.

Marita O'Neill

**

Traveling at drunken speeds, light moves
through a window, water, glass, covers
the afternoon table with a blanket of white,
transforming erasure into a presence,
leaving us sensing the passing through,
always listening in the silence as if we could hear
its creak like the weight of a foot on the stairs.

Marita O'Neill

Signatures

It was a humid city day after school
And we raced to the spot, stood staring
(a half-circle of fourth graders) at the chalk
outline of Jimmy Maguire's dad, or what
on a sidewalk was left of a man shot
and collapsed like the tail of a star—violent
and fading into the night, calling out
to those who watched—Look, a man fell here.
We crept as close as we dared, staring
inside the white lines that traced the vastness
where a red stain throbbed on the cement—
the only piece of him left behind, flowing like a secret
from his heart's last rage. We leaned in,
wanting to get closer, to dip our fingers
in the wet darkness he left behind like the mark
we're all called to make on the earth or sky,
where now, over thirty years later, a troop
of starlings expands into tall loops and cursives
as if they were spelling out the names of the air,
sun, and sky—these signatures a language
that ghosts our lives like the shape
of a man killed by his ten-year-old son
as he beat his wife for the last time.

Marita O'Neill

Heaven

In the third grade, we believed in a holy trinity:
Jesus, Sister Rita, and Steven Budgelowski's badness.
Once a week, Sister Rita, who was married to Jesus, threw
Budgey in the trash can, *where he belonged*, she'd say.

At ten, he laughed like a gambler. Crooked teeth, buzz
hair cut with a horny cowlick, only the right corner
of his mouth lifted when he smiled. He'd stick his
chest out when we called him Pig Pen, wearing it

like a war medal. One morning, she caught Budgey
hiding, eating little recess pretzels for breakfast.
So she locked him in the closet. We watched that door
all day until the frantic twisting knob finally ceased

its spasms after math class. Budgey was
an angel, she told us, who thought he was
better than God and fell into a fiery hell.
I imagined him smiling that yellow smile

when he stood before God. Would Jesus forgive Budgey
for racing sockless and late every day to school? For
carrying a hunting knife in his pocket? He seemed
to love, the way I did, Sister Rita's black and white

world where only some angels fell, and the good
angels wore white and loved little children. That day,
we saw the dead rise when she opened the closet
and Budgey, undone shirt, strutted with sweat-soaked

hair acting like he'd been at the movies all day,
a bright red ring around his mouth from eating
all the Red Hot Dollars & cinnamon Fire Balls
in Sister Rita's private stash. His pockets stuffed,

I remember how his eyes flashed, pinned on her,
the way Sister Rita told us the angels looked
when God sent them down with plagues and locusts—
how he stared at her and did not wipe his eyes.

Marita O'Neill

Notre Dame at 6 A.M.

It is too early in the morning for light
to make its way through the slender windows,
their tall frames standing over the people
like huddled trees, their stillness

communicating without words a stoic grandeur.
Once in church when I was a child, I imagined
the divine might be the robin that flew in
just as Father Ward lifted his arms to change

bread into body, wine into blood. Bold orange,
its panting and pleated chest swooped over us,
finally perching on the Virgin Mary's crown.
The hard frown from Sister Catherine told us

to concentrate on the mass, to ignore the sleek,
magic way the wings coasted above us, the way
the bird, in its distress or victory, found the ledge
of a sealed window and began to sing, its rolling

whistle dissolving all the formality around us,
drawing our laughter into its world of flight,
awaking a certain kind of joy
only a living thing carries in its breast.

Now, the sun draws back the darkness
from the scalloped windows, and light pierces
the unfolding pedals and radiant blue of the glass,
as if all those medieval artists had heard a certain music,

its sound so sweet— half angel, half human,
they used their hands and tools, twisting hot lead
to bind intricate patterns of glass, making a passage
between heaven and earth, an entrance

like a wing's sudden miracle of feathers,
unfolding before our eyes a symmetry of color
and shape so perfect and familiar,
something inside us flies.

Marita O'Neill

The Preparation

The doctor left an orange feeding tube
dangling from her nose. It snagged on
her pillow, the bathroom spigot.
He told us: if your mother loses
weight, she won't make it.
We gave her brownie sundaes,
greasy pizzas and ice cream shakes,
but she only nibbled. The doctor
said: spots on her lungs, radiation
for nine Wednesdays. Her yellow
paper kimono flapping open
in the back, she took my arm
and teetered down the hallway
venerable Mamasan, I teased.
She read St. Agnes' visions
cover to cover, and waking
from her naps, she'd tell me,
I just saw my mother and
dreamed all of you
around me as babies.

Those days she walked
the rooms on her tip toes,
as if having trouble staying
on the planet. We bought her
blue socks with suction grips
so she wouldn't go.

Marita O'Neill

Cicada

After seventeen years of sessile silence,
insatiable need for light calls them.
Hundreds of cicadas answer prehistoric clocks
that pull them out of crusted ground.
Blind eyed, they crawl from roots of white birch.

Bark under claws, sun penetrating husk,
they turn toward sky of leaves.
Clenching skin of tree, they split their backs open,
uncurl their wet, stained-glass wings, and take flight.

Sibilant cicadas screech, clutching
and climbing the city porch screen;
the day too hot to do anything but sit
and listen to the hissing heat rise and fall.
I read that female cicadas have no voice,
yet, voice or no voice, they must know
in the intuitions of their skins

     to split open from the back,

       slough their shells,

         and head for the light.

Marita O'Neill

The Howling

Summoned by a sound in the dark
Colorado hills, I stood with my mother & father
under a sky full of stars, glad to leave the walls
of our hotel room, with its cigarette-staleness
and nondescript everything confined
and more obvious than their anger
and the drinking that tore at us back then.

Unsettling, it was a sound we had never heard
and couldn't define—not quite human
and eerily human all at once—it was
growing louder and deeper, moving through
the formidable outline of hills around us.
We stood listening without speaking or arguing
for almost an hour (or was it only minutes?),
letting that strangeness fill us, bewilder us.

It was the sound of crying children, high-pitched
and filled with mourning. No, it was women
keening like wild animals as if their own hearts
were torn into pieces unrecognizable. Or it was
the mountains unburdening their weight to the sky.

I still hear that sound sometimes gathering
and feel its chill on my skin—still wonder
whether it was wolves, and still can't say. But if
that part of us which walks like a stranger
through the world, bearing its misery—lonely
and familiar—could cry out, then it might
sound like that; it might wake us in the chambers
of the heart and draw us out into the night to listen.

Marita O'Neill

New York, Afterward

Even after the rain, even one
month later—dust in the roots,

on the leaves, on the soles of my
shoes.   Even a jewelry store emptied

inside for what the people thought
was the next day's business—

looking in from the window,
gray was everywhere—glass counters,

registers, padded seats, carpets
covered but no footprints.

What stories do our bodies know
in the intimate catacombs of our cells?

Breath to word, word to prayer, ashes to ashes.

Marita O'Neill

Fancy Feast

Yesterday morning fear in my shoes
for a day I can't do, debt, middle-age, a house
I'll never pay off, I want to scream at my wife
I'm not just an unwashed cup by the sink
a bulky presence in the kitchen at a bad time.

She calls after noon, says the cat strayed
directly to her. She took him inside, called
the vet's, the shelter, the neighbors. No one
knows him. She puts him on the porch,
he cries to come in, our cats chase him
to the third floor of the house next door.

We review our liturgy. Next call he's sleeping
on the recliner after eating everything offered.
Next day the vet says, six/seven months old,
the sneezing should go away now he has a home.
Her phrase "...less stress on his system"
becomes a Latin hymn filling my head.

But he fights the shots, the blood
being drawn. The vet says he is so young
his cry is belief his mother can still help.
Between tests I hold him, his purr returning
then escalating to a beatific Gregorian chant.
At home I open a can of *Fancy Feast*.

He eats slowly, like an old woman
in the rear of the church saying her Rosary.
Eucharistically solemn he licks the plate
as though aware of the great gift that is food
then moves underneath my desk, an ancient man
returned to the cave until it's time to worry again.

Soon his body will believe, the wilderness go out
of his eyes. In this small way we seize the world
of Hume's feeble deity who abandoned us as error.
Tonight the great primal wail of the Universe
has stopped as pets and people all sleep
in the same safe place at least this one time.

Kevin Sweeney

So This Is It?

Sven walks past with a bird in his mouth
as though there were nothing between us -
all those years just thrown away.

"Hi, Sven" I try,
but he's as indifferent as the tides.

Sven's living the rich gay life,
another middle-aged man w/o kids
free to splurge on himself.
He moved in with Jesse & Jeff up the street
because their cats outate most American children
living below the poverty line.

Every night plates of lamb, chicken, beef, mixed grill
plus they left the door open all the time.
Soon Sven figured it out; what's one more for dinner
when you live/love to entertain?

At first they would bring him home regularly,
but he would howl, run down cellar and look for a window
to claw through.

We'd struggle to keep him in all night, like
a family riding it out with their drug-addled son
but in the morning he'd go back up the street and sit on
their porch

Still it hurts when we pass on the street and... nothing

It was like that girl I picked up in a bar 35 years ago.
She was gorgeous and had no business being with a practically
virginal fat boy like me

even so, we had a few dates then one night I borrowed a friend's
apartment and plied her with *Iron City* beer but

Kevin Sweeney

sex was still like trying to connect the DVD to the VCR
then the TV. I knew it could be done,
but that I'd have to muddle around first

She never gave me an explanation the night she walked
away to another guy in the same bar
He was much better looking so I wanted to say, okay,
I understand you belong with him and not me,

but why not him in the first place?
Why did you have to go out with a fat kid who still lives at home
and tear up his spongey heart?

Instead I asked, "I take it you have a ride?" but her
look of disgust suggested I wasn't very good at drawing inferences
and probably shouldn't be a philosophy major.

Today when I turned my head to follow Sven he went under a parked car
and never looked back once,
not with a nostalgic glance or pained expression of
I'm sorry but this is who I am...

Instead he kept walking.
Knowing my hope of getting him back was equal to the bird's
chance of resuming flight
I kept walking too.

Kevin Sweeney

The Comedian

My first wife never laughed at anything I said
except you can't have more money

My second wife laughs at all my jokes
emails me from work & says

two people called out sick
send me a funny message
make me laugh

So I do

I'm 54 now and my wife is 42.
When we started I was 39 and she was 27
We were ooo la la all the time

We still get ooo la la on Saturday afternoon
or Sunday when it's not football season

but my wife never sends me an email saying
I'm coming home right now;
you have to fuck me.

Instead she wants to laugh
wants me to take my finger and tongue,
turn down the lights and oh baby make it

a good one. And even though I'm my own material,
don't get any help like Letterman & Leno,

I do it every time. Mama, don't you love it.
I do, I do, yes yes, she says.

We've been together 15 years
& I keep getting funnier
& funnier.

Kevin Sweeney

Vacations

*poem written in response to the question why I'm leading a group of students to Mexico on
spring break while another group goes to Ireland "since after all, you're an Irish guy."*

The town was Drogheda, a name that soaked in ale might turn
to music, but the couple on the church steps hadn't come to sing
or pray, only to share a cigarette wet with mist. Inside: the shrunken
head of Saint Oliver Plunkett preserved by what brew I couldn't
say though Irishness would keep him dead a long time.

As those Sid & Nancy kids moved off into the nothing night of twenty
years ago, I re-boarded the bus to the colorful, the quaint & finally
Penn Station, America, home where I would marry the wrong woman,
sitting now beside me doomed as I & they at dusk by the Irish Sea.

New one on me - the only Plunkett I know plays for the Raiders,
I said - An Irishman's joke, delivered without mirth and making
no one laugh, just one more lunge at fate in a place where bad luck
loves its mirrors. We should have parted then in the land of partings

& hunger but took what passed for love in lean times in the capital
of learning to live with less. Six months before the wedding a
first marriage was dying. Lambs in Connemara had a better chance.

I need to be Irish someplace else than home, this winter's vacation
planned for the South with my second wife in the bright heat of the
Yucatan whose Catholic Church speaks a Mediterranean tongue &
caresses the stations of the cross with an Indian touch.

What's called the strand in Ireland is *playa* here.
Cognates make the case. Who wants to end in rain?
I'll choose the turquoise and silver offered by stiff brown hands.
Too much north keeps blood from the heart.

Of course, I'll go back again but not to die of white skin & gray
sky outside Dingle, believing peninsulas bring epiphany
like wind to those locked in stone. Let me finish in the sun,
fighting the claims of fog, trying in the years ahead
to once or twice just dance.

Kevin Sweeney

Sacraments

I know the invisible
parts of my body
are a darkened back stage
where props and furniture
are moved about
by earnest hands.
Likely in such human confusion
something composed of glass
will fall & break unheard
but the show will go on
without discovery until
the penultimate scene
when improvisation begins
& the narrative's movement
forward becomes everything.

Thirty years ago tormented
by the absence of women,
of tenderness I became
a devotee of pain.
Now fortunate in love
only a few topics matter
all different words for God.
Every morning
my two 13 year old cats
return to the porch
I know I have
received a sacrament.

In these Northern summer months
I swim like a solitary communicant
long distances in water so cold
almost everyone remains on shore.
They credit me with heart
& perseverance.
I want to tell them I am
those old cats sitting
on the dawn railing
liking my chances
the door will soon open.

Kevin Sweeney

I Could Have Killed Him

I hold the rear of the stroller, someone else the front.
We are carrying you on the ferry to Peaks Island.
It is low tide. Your mother and I are still married.
Neither has remembered to buckle the strap.
You could have fallen 15 feet, struck your head.

The riptide at Scarborough Beach pulled me out.
A young boogie boarder let me hold on. Unaware
the sea has rules, we obeyed them unwittingly,
kicked to the left then rode big waves to shore like floats
in the homecoming parade. I watched you reach the beach
relieved I would die alone, but how terrible for you that I'd go
first day of August, my month of custody in those days of war.

When the brakes gave on the Saab, I downshifted into second,
took a right that ran uphill & drifted to a final stop. It could have
been you traveling I-95 south from your girlfriend's dad's house
in Topsham.   I'd have been left saying if people didn't get divorced
dads wouldn't live in distant towns, and you would still be here.

Now you are twenty, impatient with phone calls, gone to college
far from home and the fear of riptide that wakes me sweating
in the night. Of course, you're okay when you don't answer for
two days; studying, drinking, wooing the half-Chilean girl
I know will break your heart again. But you don't understand
it wasn't my fault I didn't buckle you into that stroller, that

I'm sorry all these years for what I could have done; that day at
the beach it's you taken by the tides and me windswept, shivering
at dusk, a blanket around my shoulders, as the interviewer quizzes me
for TV so later viewers say aloud the names of the Holy in a tone that
could be cursing or only the tiniest, empathetic utterance of prayer.

Kevin Sweeney

Lucky

She will always only want a guy who is not you;
You are young and think not smelling her hair is
like being condemned to a wheelchair, a life of no
senses, her caramel arms never around your neck

Next someone says beauty doesn't matter.
You try to believe, knowing beauty isn't everything
for Man the Rational Animal, but you are not rational,
just an animal and want long legs, flesh that shows when
her top rides so high knees forget you're standing.

You try not to think of this when someone mentions
shallow, having convinced them you are deep, a disembodied,
contemplative skein of energy hovering above the corporeal
though secretly all you want is to live and you can't live without
her tho she seems to be doing fine without you.

In time you add beauty to your own face and frame,
a hirsute subdivision of brick and hard wood built
on a harsh terrain, and someone lets you touch her skin
so you will give her your car, your house, all the sperm
you've been saving like a 401K that you wish to withdraw
early and spend here, take the tax hit now, then you
come upon her unexpectedly - maybe in the grocery store

- and say *hey baby, wanna get lucky?* After all
those years as a monk, making jam, reading, playing
with yourself when the abbot isn't watching, you hear her
say *yes, ummm, okay, sugar, I know you're shallow, that beauty
is everything albeit short-lived so take off your clothes,*
you pay attention because someday you'll need memory,

an old car on a cold morning you want to ride
to a time when veins were full of blue and the earth lay
with one knee up wearing a dangerous, irresistible green.

Kevin Sweeney

After Attending the First 60th Birthday Party of a Contemporary

My father, his heart dead
would say he was only waiting
for it to get late enough to go
to bed alone. At one I'd take
the paperback from his hand
and kill the light. By four
he'd be up before the world
that interested him less.
On February week nights
I go to bed early, relieved
of Maine's dark cold, shut off
my wife's radio, take up a book.
He liked novels & history,
his son novels & philosophy,
understanding at last why
the old tire of the dark, would
rather sleep than stay in it
knowing how much awaits; it's
better to wake hungry for dawn
but Saturday night I give the dogs
a late run on the beach, mix
SNL with *Austin City Limits*,
read a magazine story of a young
girl studying dance in New York.
The cats all home, my son at college,
I stay up this one night to drink
green tea, knowing sometimes
it's important to fight sleep like
dying, to look at circles of light
in the living room and kitchen,
knowing it's almost over,
that it's all, it's enough
for now.

Kevin Sweeney

6 O'Clock Mass

I tell the curious
it is a mass for sinners
no one dresses the part
costumers have been banished from the temple
prostitutes occupy the street corners
by the small laundromat where the destitute
stare at nothing until ridden
by instincts to the neighborhood
store full of beer, cigarettes and canned goods:
people who would send Nietzsche
to the mountains; they must be overcome.
Good Republicans who watch the news
on channel six donate them clothes:
"Coats for Kids" - better titled "Coats for
Kids You Wouldn't Let Play With Your Kids."

It remains a gamble. That could be
Pascal sitting alone in the shadowed quadrant
two aisles away. Plenty of empty seats.
Gays are welcome here; some even extend
the collection basket or serve as
Eucharistic ministers, that Protestant innovation
of progressive Catholics too evolved for shame.
But epiphanies are hard to come by and when I
leave I'll stop at *Blockbuster* for a Sunday night
movie, something with plot to distract the mind.

I come every week and never talk
to anyone who might ask why.
Fear of oblivion is enough
to make me circle the block
a second time to find parking.
On good nights something happens:
a visiting Jesuit speaks of Kierkegaard,
a missionary evokes the atavistic heart of sympathy.
I'm simply too old to bear up under Schopenhauer

Kevin Sweeney

the god of Spinoza reminds me of an ATM machine
the priests of my childhood never grabbed my dick
the middle class went to Mass this morning then home
to dinner and prepare now for a teleological sleep

and though I love occasionally
the poor, the lame, the variously dirty-dealed
mostly I am selfish. I come here the loneliest
man in the universe. When I leave at ten minutes
before seven, sometimes I am better.

Kevin Sweeney

Liberation Theology

He doesn't look like a drunk
or Port Authority crazy
a fat belly guy with no ass
so his jeans hang low
but his cart has two bags of cans
he pushes down the street by the courthouse
where no one can park since 9/11.

I've just spent $27 and change on two CDs
at Bullmoose Records on Middle Street and
look at him the way everybody looks at a cripple
before they realize they're looking at a cripple
and that's not fair.

When I go around the block I don't yet
have a plan, but pull out my wallet and find two ones
& a ten; two fives would have covered guilt and gas
but this is when the Catholic horsepower
gives me a V-8 soul.

"You make a living doing that?"

"I do okay," he says, sounding like a guy who sells
recliners at trade shows.

"Will this insult you?" I show the ten out the window.

"Thank you, sir," he says, sounding like my son the
time I didn't ground him after finding a six-pack in the trunk.

You can't call it altruism, skeptics say,
if it feels good and esp if you talk about it to someone else

but after all, in America
who ever reads a poem
like this one.

Kevin Sweeney

No Chance

Tonight from the kitchen while eating scalloped potatoes
my second wife makes from a package, I watch the
Governor's Inauguration from Augusta. The poet
laureate of the state reads a poem about living in a house
in the woods, a magical place for children to grow up.
He has a big Bohemian beard but wears coat & tie,
like a homesteading poet dressed up with friendly
eyes and a pleasant voice for a pleasant poem.

One day I might be governor. Lunatics can run and even
win, but I will never be poet laureate of Maine. I have no
strong, silent words for the Augusta Civic Center. My family
has a gene for bad luck. I never went to live in the woods;
the woods came to live in my house. Most of my big
decisions were wrong and expensive, but

I won't take the pipe or crash the car so my son
can get insurance money to open a sporting goods store.
The governorship might still be mine then I could appoint
the poet laureate - a guy with broken capillaries in his face,
blue nose and pale hands from sitting in bars drinking
beers full of promise at the head. I'd get him up at the
inauguration with his nasal, dangerous, unstable voice
suggesting when you return to the woods the house will have burned
and raccoons are pissing on smoking mattresses.

He'd read some rambling incantatory piece about eating head
cheese, finding shit stains in his underwear & angry colon polyps
howling like starving huskies on a moonless night in the dark canal
of the human asshole and oh the winter lasts so long it makes
you crazy, no Still Life With The Wood Stove for him; yes, the
new governor is going to take a month off, head for Florida;
sure, we're looking at another budget shortfall and Gov. Sweeney
knows it will hurt, but we'll find somebody to stick it to who
won't see it coming and life, government, those of us gathered
here tonight will go on as we always have and call it a plan.

Kevin Sweeney

Grace

In the Brigham and Women's Hospital I visit my sister
with gloves, scrubs, mask, hands washed red, avoiding
germs like the taint of sin. On a better day before chemo

she confided of sending for the priest, confessing years of horror
and waste, the neglect of her immortal soul. Now it rests comfortably
in a room exorcised of soiled air while sores grow in her mouth.
My hip has been harvested for marrow which drips into her like grace.

I should tell the doctor: if you're taking from my side, why not fix
everything, make a new woman, healthy and freshly-minted with a
craving for pectin. Were our father alive, I'd complain, she always
wants what's mine. The nurses say she's at the edge, but that's normal.

Her marrow is gone and mine has moved in like a garish stranger
in a small New England town. It will have to seek acceptance:
learn to rise early, pray with the folk, send children to school
loved & well-fed, overcome the short-lived aloofness of antibodies.

No one talks how it won't work. How she'll go back to her children
and put on routine not like a house dress but a miraculous gown,
fussing to make it look right before the mirror. When she'll die in a
hospital near home, I'll remember the priest: That's it? she'd asked.

Twenty years and all forgiven? I don't have to check in once a week
like probation? Dicta don't arrive from Rome outlining my penance?
If two buses come, I bypass the local and its myriad visitations?
The one marked Express is for me?

Kevin Sweeney

My Name Should Be Theresa

"Do not believe I am swimming in consolations."
St. Therese of Lisieux

I got the news off the radio at noon:
two women from Iran joined in one
head had died on the table.
I remembered the smile of the one
always facing the camera on CNN
and was sad the rest of the day
because the universe is such a terrible
casino that the House always wins

I want to talk to Simone Weil about this.
I want Mother Theresa to tell me why
I should follow her around Calcutta
wiping the brows of lepers.

I want to know St. Therese's mind in its final
moments; was she offering the holocaust
of her 24 yr old intellect
a jury nullification of common sense
darkness flooding the lungs
while her ovaries sang like birds at first light?

Would she still have had faith at 25?
Who says you can't have a Dark Night of the Soul
in the middle of Daylight Savings Time?

They seemed like such nice ladies.

Kevin Sweeney

The Stream

"And the mouth of the person who last told all this is still warm."

— Grimm

Following Spring's muddy S
beyond the forest of peach trees,
the fisherman saw a bright crack
split rock.
He crawled through
and stood upon a narrow shelf
high above
a deep green secret
called "Amenia,"
"From the Latin," he was told,
"meaning 'pleasant to the eye:'"
barking dogs, farms crisscrossed by streams.
The happy people there
once fled a long-forgotten war.
They welcomed him, but warned:
"It's not safe nor kind to speak of us to any."
After many barbeques, kisses and handshakes,
he promised, again, to keep their valley secret,
and finally left for home, settled back into the suburbs:
the neighbors riding by on bikes
stare,
but none wave,
mow their grass
every 3 days, play
a little golf,
and bang a playground in. Years later,
drowning in debt, chewing Dentyne,
he thought he'd lead investors
back upstream —
just business: "Today given, tomorrow sold."
But spring floods
make a dozen streams,
and change every landmark.
"If Earth is 1, and Heaven's 2,"
this story could be true:
the laughing M.S. kid, longing to be free,
stumbles from his keeper,
but we
love cash.

Don Moyer

The Sea Serpent

Of all the creatures aswim through History,
the sea serpent's best,
wrapped round a rock
at the World's very edge
for her morning shower,
wrapped round a frigate,
center of the sea,
just for fun,
nudging the Plug
in the Ocean's Deep Floor,
just to be curious,
seen for a moment
from a half-remembered shore,
which rang with flags and sun.
For children, delighted,
she's real, a favorite illustration
from their Wonder Books.
But grownups,
be careful,
if you choose to catch her
in poetic nets:
use your smoothest-writing pen,
like some hopeful, just-married kid —
out there,
shoeshine and a smile,
long hair, tie and jacket: a salesman
riffing at The Two Guys
Discount Store,
delighted ("as a young dragon snapping at maidens")
to write an order for
a big commission, lemon,
Vornado TV,
sold
six times before.

Don Moyer

The Way to Cold Mountain

I seem laid back —
it's an act.
Half the time
I'm ready to blow.
Let me find
the way to Cold Mountain,
cool down
on its heights.
Han Shan, our minds
will never be the same.
Please,
the path above the trees,
rotted boards for bridges,
or half
a tree trunk,
flat side down.
You cross the misting gorge
on the slippery round.
And crossing the stream at El Paso,
coming out of Mexico,
my friend, Dave,
unbeknown to me,
had enough speed
stuck in his pants
to blast you and me

          past   Mars   .

All it took
was just one look,
but the guard
let us pass.

Don Moyer

Anniversary Snowfall

Traveling though the winter mountains
where everyone speeds
and Lao-tzu,
the waiter
at some little spot,
carries a white towel
over his left arm,
harkening back
to an older school of manners.
"Wei wu wei," say the wipers
to the falling snow —
doing not-doing —
thoughtlessly,
but my sweetie's far south
and the road's slippery;
it requires strict attention —
log trucks on my tail,
nuts in S.U.V.'s
who won't believe
anyone could be
alone,
coughing in a corner,
or stuck in a chair,
sandals on their hands.

Don Moyer

The Old Poems & Stories

"Our angry words
march away on little feet,"
prim Mrs. Mahony read
to rainy school windows
and wall clock full of lead.
And we 4th graders saw
each word form, her old mouth said:
"You can't call them back —
their little feet have claws;
their tired faces,
now,
are yours,
pinched in the heart
by Old Father Time,
'and marching as to war.'
On the job we always march / in a very straight line."
Then she smiled,
just like a witch,
and put the old
Maloik
upon us,
minnow
hanging
from her mouth.

Don Moyer

Ghost Work

"In days gone by every sound had its meaning and application."
— Grimm, "The Willow-Wren"

"When the carpenter's plane grated, it said, 'Here goes! Here goes!'
If the mill wheel began to clack, it said, 'Help. Lord God! Help. Lord God!'"
The world's more alive than we may believe,
sounds of desire
and troubled pleas;
work allows
our things to speak;
when they do,
the job's done right
by someone,
maybe you.

Don Moyer

The Art of Poetry

*"He was to poke the fire under the kettles wherein the
hell-broth was stewing."*
                    — Grimm, "The Devil's Sooty Brother"

I don't like people sticking their noses in my business.
I don't like jerks who tailgate.
I don't like my arm going numb
when I take a pill
to quell
the free-floating anxiety,
and try writing something,
with the other,
to unknown people
who couldn't care less.
"All bad things I do
will go
up in smoke."
Yeah,
but I'll go with them —
just another
stupid
boiling pot of blood
and vermicelli,
made of "understandings
so fine
they're threaded in a needle."
Pasta and sauce:
my last meal.

Don Moyer

The First Blue Day of Spring

God throws open His huge right hand
and sparrows pour through spring.
"If a little time is left,
it is only a last scrap."
But sweet, so close to bone.
Our luck still holds, today —
God hasn't opened
His left.
"People wanting poems
continue to clamor
all day long,"
Yuan-mei wrote,
250 years ago.
They still clamor, but not for poems.
God, poet, or magician —
you need to watch both hands.
Again
God opens
His huge right hand;
again
a thousand sparrows lift.

Don Moyer

Home

"Every one who dwells here is safe."
                                    — Grimm

"And they lived happily, ever after."
So delicate —
the blue rug
and shell-white walls,
cedar porch,
fried chicken,
deck overlooking
summer trees.
Then
the mellow jizz
falters:
an outlaw-grey,
eastern coyote,
still fizzing from Dreamland,
takes its time,
crossing,
Farm-to-Market Road,
looking right at you,
its face,
more pointed
    than
    you
    can
    im
    ag
    in
    e
    .

Don Moyer

A List of Streets in this 1957 Town

For My 8th Grade Friend, R.B.

Straight Street
Proper Way
Grub Street
Bracken Lane
Millerton Hill
My friend, Richard Brin,
found his way in
one spring morning,
no hands, on a bike,
pulled a knife
on cool, always smiling,
Donald McDonald,
to avoid
a schoolyard beating

as everyone crowds outside to see
how easy he strips
my blade off me,
and wise guy words don't work,
when I'm hit in the face and balls by this jerk;
my face could never
be a friend's;
the girls just watch me
bleed and bend.

The sheriff drove
Richard back
to the ancient brick by brick
("I love God, real hard")
State Reform School.
He's standing, again, in his old room,
even Ritchie Valens
can't save him now,
just a bright
overhead light;
other boys look in.
Love your home;
God sees all –
every little sparrow fall,
here
on Straight & Narrow.

Don Moyer

I'm Running Out of Everything

I've spent much of life
being angry
over petty, hellish things,
counting wrongs
like tiny brass screws —
a million, two,
I spilled the glue,
running out of time,
vodka and lime.

Satan smolders on Neurontin,
right along with me:
in the thicket of details,
I sold this, you took that;
devil records every dime.

You know him:
smiling
Reddy Fox face,
finger to his lip,
carries a pointed stick,
sharp teeth,
sly connoisseur
of silent farts
and many other wrongs,
fat bag swelling
on his belt,
quite full:
slippery souls in wine;
one's mine.
He uses us
for fuel.

All the people I still hate
pretend a life
as fair and straight
as God's Finger
pointing out hell,
from His porch,
up there.

Don Moyer

Quitting Time

After dinner, clean your room,
maybe take a nap.
Awake again in fifty years
(tired of working as you slept)
among the river leaves,
where folks like us
work till 4
punch out quickly
head out the door
and into
          summer breeze

Don Moyer

'Bo

"I know I'll die alone
by the side of the road
with the gravel and sand
and stuff thrown out
as intimate friends,
and it's O.K. –
an escapee from
The Sunset Retirement Home,
just tottered out
the ringing back door
up the green hill
to Route 66
stuck out a thumb
caught a ride
right off –
a bright red
409
(Is this the past?)
but no questions asked
of the cute blonde
just happy now
to move on
top down
knowing enough, between rides,
to lie doggo,
when cops come nosing for 'bos,
and stay
an extra few minutes
flat,
(Ma Field Mouse flees, 3 babes on her back.)
I wait,
wise old Mr. Rat,
just to be sure
the boys in blue, all,
are gone.

Don Moyer

'Close to Nature, action and will,'
I head back down the Lost Highway,
faint in the crease
of a tossed-out map.
As my friend, George Blaiser, once said,
'Stick out your thumb,
but always keep moving.'"

Don Moyer

Nursing Home Rejected

"It's easy to use a gun, just don't point it at someone you like."

The old folks started a commune
instead of going back
to elementary school,
forgot those posters on the wall:
"Be a choosy chewer"
"Eat fruit and vegetables every day"
(with scenes of marching carrots and bananas.)
They liked Clapton, soft porn, strong weed,
but Our State
stepped in,
produced a botched-up shoot-out
for six o'clock news.
Four things left
in the clearing dust:
a red checked shirt,
a red baggy dress,
a postcard from The Everglades,
a warm
22.
No mercy
but God's
I.O.U.

Don Moyer

Dad's Bread Bowl-Ceramic

It has a crack inside,
For that matter
It continues outside.
That huge crater helped create
Floured and yeasty treats
For a generation.

The chip on the rim
Might have been
A hurried put away
For a quick escape into
The rarity of snow.
The bowl was more a pantry
Than any item in a pantry.

This barren bowl has not felt
The warmth
Or expansion of dough, nor
A cover towel that hid
Such mystery since dad
Died autumns ago. The click
Of his watch to that ceramic
Edge, is now only a faint echo
Of my past.
It doesn't matter what the results;
Rolls were gobbled, scratch cakes
Devoured, bread, buttered and swallowed.

Dad hit us all, some said out of love, others
Will not speak about it. And bread cannot rise
Without loving hands.
This bowl of plenty sits on a Kitchen Queen
In the dining room, holding seasonal fruits.
Why they rot quicker there than on a counter
Is not a mystery to me.

Tom Delmore

Dad's Gift

He gave me deer skin gloves
Smooth and supple, deceptively warm.

I took the gloves
And used them
For all the wrong things
Deer skin dried
Thread broke and unraveled.
Useless, except to shove
On a cluttered closet shelf.

I still have his
Woundings, the gloves
No match for that type of storm.

Tom Delmore

Wind Place

The wind coming through my window
Is from my grandma's farm
A childhood past.
It comes as summer sun,
Or fog in fall.
Through my half-open mind
That always dreams.

Mom's naked back pointing
To a tick. Partial window
A shade could not cover,
Looks onto unused pasture.

The wind says: "write me down
So I may live on and on."

The kitchen where Uncle Napoleon
Ate peas with a knife. Dry lightning
Like my dry alcoholic dad
Scattered violence everywhere, making
The skyline pink and faces red.

Tom Delmore

Final Meal

For Katherine Dyckman

I sit waiting
Not my turn
But only two chairs.
In love
Food is brought
To aged hands.
Burnt toast
Poached egg
Thin sliced ham
In between.

Before I was born
They ate this meal.
The light from the lake
Not yet part
Of their
Intimacy.
One hand free
The other to hold.

It is cut in squares.
A ritual
Honoring sustenance.
No wasted portion --
Only now
He forgets
Who the maker is
And she loves him
Too much to tell.

Tom Delmore

Occasion of Sin

I said a rosary for you
too confused,
burning a candle at both ends.
You talk and I can't
dribble out a joyful mystery.
I feel your pain and grief
and can't help holding
beads between my fingers.
I die a little
with each decade
and can't say goodbye
or a decent glory be.
I know my words
are an occasion of sin
but I do love you.

Tom Delmore

Rail Yard Blues

When dad crossed those tracks
His imagination went.
The vibrations stole him away.
He could chicken dance over the rails
Sucking steam and diesel.
The glory train that took his future
Was creosote on the cuff of his pants.

Tom Delmore

Questions to a Panhandler

If I give you some
what will I give the others?
were you not on forty-seventh
with that make-shift sign?
Now it's forty-third
and your rent is not enough
paid up to stay indoors?
And what of the two
nameless children on the sign,
are they on forty-fifth
or are they inside
the folds of your coat?

Did city officials design
the narrow of street
that I had to trip,
turn, feel concern
for your hunger, the rent
the children, and a way
of escape for me?

Tom Delmore

Frida Full of Milagros

I want to hold hands
With Frida, and place
My index finger between her
Publicly pubic eyebrows.
Like crow wings stamped
For flight.
Slip myself into her widespread
portrait, and kiss her full
on her radiant red mouth.
All this below the Infant
of Prague.

Sit like a skeletal couple
At the Ramos wedding
As lovers
Eat bright fruit
Off our ample laps.

Out of the oculus
Fascination arises
For the voluptuous sister
In partial undress,
As one might lust for mangos.

Tom Delmore

Anything Good

The back porch --
did anything good
come that way?
Sacks of sprouting potatoes,
hoes, rakes and shovels.
Smells,
to kill weeds, ants,
spiders and mites.

The back porch --
did anything good
come that way?
Alley friends
came up red steps
to enter.
Mom, hands on hips
wondering if kids ever go
to their homes.
Their names were:
"Wipe your shoes,"
"hang your coats up,"
"not the dog," and
"can't you play at Danny's house?"

The back porch --
did anything good
come that way?
I carried my father
dying through that space
and placed his blood
stained sheets by the door,
hovering in mom's cry:
"burn these now!"

The back porch --
does anything good
come that way?

Tom Delmore

Crows on Winter Solstice

Right before dusk
A murder of crows flies east
From well-tilled earth.
When this mood to move
Takes over, they chasm
Into chaotic flight.

Above the conifer and over
The next hill.
Hidden, black on black
They rejoice
In the darkest day of the year.

Tom Delmore

Crow Myth

Crow knows bear
from a distance.

In another time
crow resided
on bear's back
roaming hard
curvaceous muscles.
Fighting or mating
crow would flit
to tree or shrub.
Crow loved the rolling
indentation of bear.
Crow would cling
to the upper trap area,
whispering nonsense
and ill advice.
Bear thought
it was natural chatter.

Bear was certain
crow had always been
part of her physique.
Never controlling
but adjusting to
crow's intentions.

In one moment, and one
moment only,
crow became dislodged
from bear when thrown
from its perch
by a mounting male.
Crow's broken wing
made bear ever curious.

In devouring crow
bear became crotchety.

Tom Delmore

Jamison's Opera House after Intermission

The usher has closed
the door, the music
begins. A rustle
of feathers or is it
fingers on a silk lapel,
a handsome man appears
all black except for
a twisted piece of wax paper
in his beak.

The usher leans
to reopen the door
only to find
two individuals
scuffling over this waxed
bauble.

the usher gestures
by flaying his arms
dispersing the triad
to the foyer and out
a transom
        blinking: No Exit.

Tom Delmore

Infant of Prague, Circa 1960

The statue stood
On a window sill
Hidden by a transparent
Curtain.
The color of the figurine was
Harvest gold
Orange and white.
Like a guardian
It watched over
A family
Of rosaries --
Wood, plastic, silver
Glow-in-the-dark.

When the statue was brought down
And placed on an oval table
For a feast or to remind
This Irish family that God
Appears in all forms,
It was dreadful.

At some point the infant
Lost its head, crown, cross,
And royalty.
It could have been by clumsiness
Or being held
At the same spot over the years.
Glued so many times
The neck was a collar
Of brown goo.

Tom Delmore

How Far is Safe?

There is a flicker
When eyes squint
To block out
War images on the screen.
As if
The dead dance and dart
In the video stream.
Maybe a mother holds
A foot, attached to nothing,
Or carries a child
Without a face.

We are a safe distance
From Baghdad, and put
Our feet into shoes
And carry our smiles
And walk down busy streets.

Jolted (God forbid)
By terror
That lifts through
Plate glass, and mannequin
Stares.
A chuckle erupts
From inside
As you hold
your new balance
Foot inserted
Leg missing.

Tom Delmore

MIA

Copper corrodes the wrist
marking time in green stains.
Near fifty years
Some soldiers
have not come home
sons of farmers
dying to see
sons of magicians
dying to see
sons of the deceased
dying to see
sons of ex-priests.
The list goes on
but they don't.

Twisting copper deep
makes it bleed
reminds one of a just
cause with muddled ends.
Moments in the flash
detonate the flesh.
Bring them home
what is left
buried under white stones
call their mothers
three wars past
and say the boys' odds
were in their favor
to visit an exotic land
and spill blood
on distant soil.

Tom Delmore

From the Greek

You have to be careful what you
say around here. You

might say *come with me,*
flatten the cool grass with your body
and stare a hole into the sky
when what you really mean is
fuck you. The past is a language unto

itself — a great pasture,
hewed by the path of us.

And that warm spot in the pool?
It is nostalgia, that bundt cake of desire and pain.
Nostalgia, from *no,* you'll never be in that church
again, wearing the dress
with lace fingers swirling up your chest,

a church made for playing basketball
with thick lines painted on the floor.
But we were there,
our toes behind the foul line
taking a shot at it. Taking a chance.

And from *stal,* as in
never again will you do that in the bathroom stall
of the Madison High School gym
during a boxing match, a string
of saliva and blood, the cocktail of pugilism
dripping from the open mouth of the boy in the silver trunks.

Never. He flushed
before you walked out
into that maze of ceilingless conversations,
the model of your very own heart, that
complicated chapel.

Michelle Lewis

Like those pews, those fingers running down
the page full of verses, over John, Paul, and sweet Peter,
every need is its own meadow.

And *gia* as in, what will make us whole -gia?
-Gia, -gia, you syllabic godlette,
will you be our caretaker into the next round?

As in -gia, that baffling girl,
because there has to be someone
sidesaddling it into the ring, whispering
undecipherable things to her knees.
Someone to cry for no reason at all.

Michelle Lewis

The history of the world

The day has darkened your hair.
It is beautiful the way you carry
the whole world around with you:

dirt from the street where you walked
      looking for the city's
            best enchilada, your skin's own oils,
your body always
compromising itself.

Every day ends with this:
a coil of words
      around a face.

Today a man smiles, fires a gun
into his life's air, possibility blossoms,
      splays,
          a Fairfield clinic burns.

The body remembers yesterday's heavy lifting.

When I hear some do not survive, I
      cannot stop holding you, afraid the moon
      sees everything at once.

Blood circles the nut of our hearts
while our lives gather, papers pile and are taken away
      given the right physics
we are weightless.

Across the street
a bulb's bald eye burns on its cord
inside the old man's garage,
an ant at its task, he is
building something beneath its glow. The sky is loose, alive,
      a silence buzzes inside.

Michelle Lewis

Planes rise from the runway
angle off
             until they can no longer be seen

and every day ends with you.

             I want to tell you I am grateful
that we are perfect and
consequential, but I can't believe how frail
                        multitudes can be

while webs in every corner
bow under their weight
held together by sheer science, by fantastic
                        legends of strength.

Michelle Lewis

Looking for Bo Derek

I am peering through the trees in the public park, which,
because it's October and the leaves have mostly fallen, means
I can see more than I ever could before beyond the branches
there, and there it is, what you would call a promenade wrapped
around a monstrous house like a belt around some very large woman's
waist, that then culminates in a roomy circular porch all white
and elegant like something from *Architectural Digest* or the set of *Dynasty*,
which is a show that I remember, full of shoulder pads and big
hair starring Linda Evans who was married once to John Derek
who then married Bo Derek, the bronze, braided beauty whose
real name is actually Mary Cathleen Collins, and who, incidentally,
looks remarkably like Linda, but if you like certain things then
who am I to say, because here I am in the park, crouching
between two trees, staring at this porch, and I can't help but
wonder about the people that live there and how happy they
must be to have little shapes carved into the wood of their
porch, and it happens that I haven't had a shower for two days
and so I am at this moment what my mother might call a
ragamuffin, which in her precisely lipsticked mouth
would hold absolutely no humor, and I sense that I am part of a
juxtaposition, but I'm working on a paper, which actually
sounds a lot better than it really is so I just haven't taken the
time for hygiene, which invariably runs into more time than it
really sounds like it should and I just hurried out to the park to
walk the dog, but the whole time I keep looking and thinking
about the house and start to figure that the people are very
likely no more happy than anyone, and it's just a porch, and
maybe they don't shower on occasion or put on clean clothes,
but who would notice in that sort of house anyway, which
looks like a place where Oprah's Book Club might meet, an
episode, actually, which I did see because I was home working
on the paper, which this time is sort of better than it sounds
because that morning some student from my class said he had
written down something that I said the other day and I couldn't
believe it because it had been one of those weeks where the
ennui had sort of taken on a life of its own, and started growing
arms and legs and walking around and growling and speaking
Latin and pulling my heart out and eating pieces of it right in
front of me so it would take every single mind trick of delusion

that I could muster to actually go in there and keep from feeling
like we all had a fatal case of the Bends, the characteristics
of which they always show in movies about the military
when you start to realize this poor sod's not going to make it,
and then I thought that this kid had written down this quote, this one
-liner that I'd been carrying around that seemed to relate in some
way to his life or maybe he wanted to use it on one of his friends
or just keep it in case something came up where he needed something
that would make him sound quippy and more interesting, and
that made me so happy that I went home and instead of
working on my paper I watched *Oprah*, and there they were
sitting outside in front of this enormous home with drinks and
passing this hardcover novel around like it was the last living
zygote of the white lynx or something, and is now probably
half-off in some bin along with *The 60-Minute Gourmet* and
Harry Connick Jr.'s second Christmas album, but now here
I am crouching, hoping someone will step out onto the porch
even though it's well into fall now, and whoever lives there
probably has a flat in the city or a condo in Florida and is
walking out on that porch, and I'm feeling a bit like Jimmy
Stewart in Rear Window except nothing's happening and I
don't know if I'm expecting Old Lady Havisham with the
wedding dress on from that day decades ago when her lover
never came and she waited and waited because she couldn't
bear the thought that he wouldn't come and if she just kept that
dress on maybe he still would, and haven't we all been there
before, I mean not with the dress and the bad makeup but
haven't we all believed in something we shouldn't, and by
now I'm hoping for just someone with jeans and a rum and
coke who's stepping out for a breath of fresh air, just
something, or maybe even old Mary Cathleen, because she
must be at least as old as Linda Evans was on Dynasty and we all
have to live somewhere, and then I start thinking that John
Derek when he met her must have figured that it's sort of nice
the way your life never turns out exactly how you initially thought
you wanted it to turn out, and how we sort of build our own houses,
and I'm thinking how you have to lean out over the porch
of your own life, you have to walk out onto that promenade or into
that room and stand there and let apathy wipe its mouth with
your own shirtsleeve, you have to say bold, beautiful, second-
hand things, just in case someone is listening.

Michelle Lewis

Penguins migrating at the San Francisco Zoo

Brainwashed by six newcomers from Ohio, 46 penguins at the San Francisco Zoo have abandoned their burrows and embarked on a great migration — except their pool is not exactly the coast of South America and there's really nowhere for them to go. [...] Now they swim most of the day and stagger out only at dusk.

—The San Francisco Chronicle

All great deceits are pill-shaped and
unquestionable.
The world must have rolled out
flat as a blade, always an arc of hope beyond
that same fake tree, same manmade island
to another spit of land, another
needle of mud or gold.
                   Once, when I was driving
a pool looked like a fjord, so I bought
a suit to swim in
and in a hotel mirror
saw the angles of my own back
scapula rising where wings would be.
It was not the bone
but what the doubled mirrors made
that I could not believe —
        that geminied sphinx,
a shouldering chorus line
beyond what I could count. When one moved,
the rest did. Such geometry twisted in that silver sea!
      All bets are off, it's chaos,
        no one knows when this will stop.
But flesh and blood, what an army you do make
              over what distance will you follow me

Michelle Lewis

The desire line

Just beyond the porch
      the walkway gleams
idle as a prince, abandoned
in favor of the desire line:
the route we'd rather take
little mudway through the grass
from pile of dropped bikes
to schoolhouse door

      or the dirt lasso
around the thicket where the dogs
pound out a circle.
It starts as the shorter way
but always meanders drunkenly
around an invisible vector
with that first navigator's ill but
pioneering sense of it

a means of getting there with passion's name.
Look – we've worn a path around our
little bed, our big TV. Every conviction
was a notion once. On ours
I dropped a pearl earring,
toted bags of trash, books and bottles.

Once, late at night, coming home, I fell there –
      then stayed, while you went on ahead
and I watched as the house lit,
first one room then the next
      like a fire stoked, then glowed from
every window. I saw the
days take shape and then the years.
I saw that everything I thought was mine
by some bequest
           was not,
was once a random sightline
designless, unheroic
and then followed.

Michelle Lewis

Starfish

You never find them floating
like you think you should:
rippling like a wind-wracked banner,
or fingering themselves onto a wet rock

       but they've got to have
an agenda, this shore is full
of their tacit courtesy, which
seems almost on the cusp
of chaos. They are quiet now, parched
and blank-faced, a spew of
tiny supplicants. But
cut off an arm
and you're just asking
for regeneration.

To them the future must seem
like the dark interior of a conch
and the past
— a flint of calcite.

I pretend so much lately.

Maybe somewhere one of them
is reaching a phalange
into the dark to translate
a rock into a map. She knows
even her namesakes were never born
to the constellations we calculated
for them.
      But they do
make the world smaller
and less baffling
      — make part of you think
even as you praise its mystery
that you could conquer it.

Michelle Lewis

The truck drivers

When I think of men, I think of their sleepy vulnerability
and hearty appetites, the crush of denim
that stacks above their boot tops,
and of the one my mother was
partial to
        for his white teeth and told him so in the kitchen, laughing
the morning after they arrived, made two shudders of
water through the pipes
and stayed in an unfinished bedroom.
                Sight unseen filled their eighteen-wheeler:
curved torsos of lamps with metal pirouettes above their bulbless heads
      cartoon cut-outs shellacked onto wood squares beveled to
         a frame, and ceramics – bloat-faced children
                    genderless as elves. We kept
a desultory clown
with a chip that I filled in
with red nail polish,
      and four plates. The rest
was priced to draw the wives of men
who came to stand, hands in yesterday's workpants,
around the Golden Hawk Studebaker and reupholstered chairs
         gathered like a stew of gaudy aunts,
         brass tacks holding in their fat chests.

They had driven most of the night.
And in the morning: flannel shirtsleeves rolled into their longjohns,
tired, hungry for eggs on a plate. If desire is a throbbing
followed by the need to drug it
      I would not have had that then. I listened to
a radio from my bed and thought about
which one I liked best, where they came from
         and where they were hauling off to, truck emptied out

and nimble, ignited by the morning. When I think of
         men, I think of the far provinces of away
where they sit and call at the crest of home and
too far gone, and how
when asked about their lives
they bend their elbows,
      search their damp, wild hair with their hands.

            Michelle Lewis

We looked at Mars

We had been cooking something wicked –
       we severed brainstems of live lobsters,
       cleavered claws so meat flowered
       from knuckled ends. They
opened and closed
and opened in the pan.
It was difficult,
yes, but it was

summer. We separated ourselves from it
long enough to eat: it was savory
and superlative
       claws the red of our shoulders,
reflecting everything. We had watched the sun

sink below the earth like a theater girl in her bejeweled skirt.
All week the anchors would not say
between what worlds the faces
of the uniformed were.
But they told us

the distance of that planet from the earth,
       closer than it would be
       again in our life.
They were shaken with the weight of that so
we were, too.

We looked so long we almost
swallowed it! Almost felt it say
       something about the world.
But we were tired and full.
We let the sky have its moment. We didn't
need to read the earth's every diary entry.

      Once, I told a student
I could accept that the sky

Michelle Lewis

was beautiful, only
if I knew one spoiled
by clouds. He wasn't buying it
due in part to the blind love
we have for our creations

so the day remained
perfect on the page, and in the end we both
crawled into it willingly.
We left our bodies to their shuffling, our pens
to their marginalia. And when the meal was over,

I felt a little like that.
Butter congealed in bowls, wicks
waited in centers to burn
while night drew a knife
              and stabbed us with its clarity.
                    Red Mars gleamed
in its quadrant. We observed
the world from all angles
out of duty, out of respect for Time, because Time

is just the baker on the night shift
fat and flopheaded
who moves among the dough and amber fig
kneads his worktable into years
and we wake up and eat those years.

We left the planet to its orbit.
We let our fears have their private death.
It took a while. But it was still early,
and warm
and we wanted it to seem
like a decision we had made.

Michelle Lewis

Dear Angie Dickinson,

the streets are full of the wounded.
I think love must be a bullet
or a seed. And yet,
      who doesn't love the frailty
of women? Recall
the mobility of that blue gabardine
pantsuit, robin's egg,
so much better than those whalebone
corsets. And Emily, that other
Dickinson, was so willingly mangled.
So quick to hyphenate
with that long diving board of
want. It was not for us.
Only a fool would trade in her hot rollers
for a meticulous bun. But you
closed your door. You slept
with the asides of men who didn't take you
seriously — *little spitfire, I bet you can do it,*
they'd wink, *you're a smart girl.*
            Angie, you never wanted
to be bent over dirt in Dixmont, Maine
selling blue potatoes at festivals.
But look at you now! It's 2002
you're playing someone's
homeless grandmother in some
new movie, fat with costume clothes —
you've got to wonder who it was
who betrayed who. I still learned it —
that knack for being heard
with one sincere *motherfucker*
and some décolletage. There is no time
but the present and I am one
of this street's bad decisions,
heart eating bullets, thumbs planting
seeds. I'm a smart girl. I should have

Michelle Lewis

figured it out – your age
out from under someone's thumb
telling the women over lunch
my ex is somebody else's problem.
Sober, or no – still sliding the glass top
from the carafe, pouring out a scotch
sliding it back with a clink.
Jaw on a swivel. Packing heat,
toughing it out. Picking up the dry cleaning,
walking through the streets, swinging
a blond curl out of an eye. Knowing
like you knew
there's no idea that's not eventually
a hand, no hand that's not eventually
a gun.
Angie, the streets are full of wounded.
I think love must be a bullet
or a seed.

Michelle Lewis

The pepper

We sliced the red pepper
open —
saw the shining nose, a tumor in the belly
which toppled out, progeny of red,
swell of asymmetry, of youth.

It trembled on the counter
— so clean —
beside what bore it.

Though we were sure enough
this was growth's lapse,
a burden to the hollow
body it had tossed in,
we agreed to
slice
and join

the tiny ear
with what had possessed it.

We watched
its knots and blooms
grow more distinct with each cut
then vanish. It was, it seemed,
just like all the others.

Had it become our creed
to have the oyster
for the oyster, the artichoke
as penance for its heart? We did not believe
that will itself held a sweeter taste

and so we ate the false self
with the self

and once gathered
made no real effort to discern it.

Michelle Lewis

I Stand at the Counter

I stand at the counter
   cooking in the convento's kitchen,
   surrounded by pots, pans,
   some dull and dented and banged,
   some bright and smooth and shiny,
   cupboards with rosemary, anise,
   local saffron and other spices and herbs,
   all pungent and nearby
   bottles of olive
   oil in shades of green
   and gold that glisten
   like the colors in Renaissance
   paintings.

Slowly, carefully, I peel
   the small Forelli pears
   my fingers sticky with
   their golden juices
   until I have twelve ready.
   I put 3 cloves in the
   bottom of each one and set them
   in the deep skillet. I put shreds
   of tangerine peel
   into the skillet with them,
   slowly drizzle in thick fragrant
   Tuscany honey, pour
   in the half-bottle of young
   Chianti and set them to simmer
   for dinner dessert tonight
   with amaretti and tiny cups
   of rich black coffee sweetened
   with squares of dark chocolate.

Kelly Lombardi

Mannion's Bar

On Tuesday, on the way back to San
  Gimignano from Torre del Lago,
  Puccini's home, we stopped at
  Casa del Mare and feasted on fish
  cooked in a spicy aromatic sauce,
  drank the local white wine—
  dry and fruity and tangy—
  with the strains
  of Tosca still capturing us.
  All around us people were
  laughing, eating, drinking,
  talking and a voice coming from
  someone at the table in the corner
  had the unmistakable Irish lilt
  of Mayo...and I remembered:

Last Tuesday, with two other friends
  we were seated in Mannion's Bar in Balla,
  Mayo at sticky brown wooden tables
  and drinking pints of Guinness
  —heavy and dark and creamy—
  while waiting for Tom Lyons
  and the JoBange band
  to get playing. All the talk quieted
  as the band began and Mike Holzer
  started strummin' and singing
  Dirty Old Town as if all the great old
  Delta blues men had risen up from their graves
  and grabbed his soul.

Too soon, too soon, the Tuesday night
  band started to put
  away their instruments and Mannion
  was bringing around baskets of chips,
  and sausage, and wings. During the first quiet,
  a sweet soprano voice from the other end
  of the bar started singing Take Me Home to Mayo.

Kelly Lombardi

One by one we joined in, quietly, reverently,
remembering. There was a minute of silence
when we finished and then Mannion called:
Drink up, folks, drink up.
It's time. It's time.

Kelly Lombardi

Sharing the Apples

Going down the cobble-
   stone hill
   to the convento,
   I stopped to buy apples,
   freshly picked,
   damp,
   and sweet smelling—
   stopped again at Gastoro's
   for a cappuccino,
   and to pet
   the old Alsatian dog—
   grey masked and stiff legged—
   who came to greet me
   daily.

We share the crisp
Biscotti di Cantucci,
and bites of apples;
I give his ears a final rubbing
before I leave
to go to Boboli's
to buy
the walnut studded
Pane di Noci for
tonight's dinner.

Kelly Lombardi

The Dogs of
San Gimignano

Dogs
walking up
and down
the cobbled street
where not a patch of
grass is to be found.

those on leashes
being tugged
and pulled
and not
allowed
to leave their mark
on the streets.

I feel
sorry for them,
but those others
who wander
without leashes
find me
sitting on the Convento
steps and come
and lean
against me
for strokes—

Some scruffy, some big,
some mini, some wire-haired,
some young and frisky,
some older
already masked,
stay and
join with me
in sympathy
for the others…

Kelly Lombardi

The Scent of Rosemary

When my winter
   shrouded house
   is covered in gray
   even the birds sound
   heavy hearted,
   as they fight wind
   currents in their
   daily search for food,
   and the sea growls
   at the fragile
   soils of the bluffs;
   Italy beckons
   with its sweet
   sun drenched
   landscapes,
   twisted vines and fertile
   olive trees.

When my spirit needs sustenance
   I long for the Convento
   Sant' Agostino,
   the simple single room
   the sheltering arms of walls
   the rosemary scented courtyard
   the frescoed chapel
   the soft sounds
   of the priests
   in their daily
   rituals.

I close my eyes and
   see it, faintly
   hear them again, and
   the sweet soprano voices
   of their sisters at the
   Eremo Agostiniano
   di Lecceto
   singing their
   noon office.

Kelly Lombardi

Sitting in the Sun

Sitting in the sun on the church steps,
  I watch one couple, Danish, I think
  leave their dog outside
  when they go into
  the trattoria.
  He sees me and wanders over, scenting
  a friend.

I reach my hand out, palm up, and he rests
  his big yellow head on it, while
  I scratch the soft silky skin of his throat
  and he makes sounds of contentment.

I cup my hands and share some of my water
  with him before he sits down and
  leans against me while we enjoy the sun
  in silent sweet communion.

Kelly Lombardi

Rain Sounds

Rain sounds different
  here, in San Gimignano,
  where it falls on tile roofs—tiles
  rounded and made by hand
  centuries ago.

From my room in the ell, I hear it:
  plunk, soosh, ping, splash, plink—
  before it slides off the roof onto the
  cobblestone street to dance
  down the hill to the porto..

If I get up and look out the window,
  I will see the persimmon tree's
  leathery leaves glistening,
  and over near the gate, the fig tree
  with its still small fruit is absorbing it

If I close my eyes, I can imagine
  the small sweet fruit ripened
  in the sun with the bees gorging
  on the sweet, sweet fruits
  dripping with nectar.

Kelly Lombardi

The Solitary Stroller

But on this wet windy cold December day,
   few other tourists are about, and I enjoy
   walking in the semi-solitude, deep
   collar of my coat turned up against
   the wind that snarls through the narrow
   ways, watching the rain run
   down the cobbled streets forming small
   rapids, seeing the shop-keepers
   huddled behind the steamed up
   windows listening to the silence of their
   cash registers and looking sadly at their wares,
   the high piles of olive oils, wines, olives, cheeses,
   leathers, and colorful pottery.

The towers glisten in the rain as if they
   have been oiled; the duomo stands forlorn
   in the piazza where all the trattorias are shut
   and the chairs piled outside Even the ever
   present pigeons are huddled in the holes
   of the church wall, their feathers fluffed out,
   their necks tucked in against the dreary day.
   I climb the steps and the door is shuttered tight.
   Slowly, I turn and walk back to the Convento,
   and go into the small church there with
   its lovely frescoes and banks of candles.

I light candles, pray and give thanks.

Kelly Lombardi

Market Day

The steep cobbled streets are wet,
  and slippery,
  as I walk up to the Piazza
  del Duomo where the vendors
  are just setting up
  their wares.

Shouts, laughter, greetings,
  resonate across the stalls
  where the freshest of fruits—
  oranges, temples, (with their stems
  and leaves still attached) apples,
  lemons, melons tempt me;
  the freshest of cheeses—fat, round,
  square, some with ropes to hang them
  makes me salivate with hunger,
  and build sandwiches in my mind
  with the dried sausages
  and fresh salad greens.

With my string bag filled with fruits,
  meats, cheeses, and vegetables
  for tonight's dinner,
  I hike across to the Trattoria,
  order my cappuccino and apple pastry,
  read the International Herald Tribune,
  chat with the other breakfasters
  in a mishmash of languages,
  with much hand gesturing,
  and a lot of smiles,
  before taking my leave,
  gathering my goods,
  and walking back to the Convento.

Kelly Lombardi

A Simple Room

A simple room,
  scrubbed and plain
  with a small white
  tiptilty table
  on which sits
  a round based white lamp
  with a weak yellow bulb
  that sheds almost
  no light,
  a single bed is
  against one wall:
  above the bed hangs an icon
  of the Black Madonna of Prague,
  against the opposite wall
  a simple wooden crucifix
  and across from the bed
  an old wardrobe looms.
And, on the bed,
  a coarse white coverlet is
  stretched with two
  starched pillow slips covering
  the lumpy pillows.
The floor is simple
  scrubbed linoleum
  some neutral shade of gray,
  and there is an old
  wooden student desk,
  scarred and chipped,
  but sweet-smelling
  from lavender
  scented polish.
In front of the desk,
  facing the window
  which has shutters
  of olive wood
  open to the Tuscany sky
  is a straight-backed chair,

Kelly Lombardi

a bit wobbly,
not too comfortable,
but it will do.
If I stand, I can see
the walnut tree,
the persimmon tree,
the tall stone wall
of our Area Privato
the tower, the herb bed,
the tall waving plants Father Jim
planted by the gate
and Camilla, the calico
cat, chasing birds below.
In the distance I see
the golden Tuscany hills
with their geometric fields
of olives and figs
and tidy red tiled roofs
of houses.
I have traveled well
and enjoyed the
lush fittings
the great city hotels
have to offer;
I have listened to world famous voices
in some of the great music halls
of the world,
But, I would rather be here
in this simple room
scrubbed and plain
and sweet smelling,
with my notebook
open on the desk,
and my warm blue shawl
thrown over the chair,
listening to
the voices of the friars
doing their noon offices
than anywhere else in
the world.

Kelly Lombardi

Plague Season

In the early oil paintings,
　　the doctors who treated the ill
　　during the plague had large
　　pointed beaks made, and
　　filled with flowers and herbs,
　　tied over their
　　mouths and noses to ward
　　off the vapours of the
　　disease.

This season, all the young
　　Italian women walking
　　the streets of San Gimignano
　　are wearing bird's
　　beak shaped boots,
　　and I wonder
　　if they are stuffing the beaks with
　　flowers and herbs, and what
　　disease it is
　　they are warding off.

Kelly Lombardi

Night Song

I listen
as the strange
screeching wind
sweeps
through the streets

up the Via San Matteo
circling the Duomo
down and around
the Piazza della Cisterna

sending leaves,
tourists' debris,
torn newspapers,
and odd bits of fruit

from the market
held yesterday
swirling
through the San Gimignano
streets
and out the porto.

Kelly Lombardi

Tuscany Light

I have come back to San
   Gimignano again to restore,
   to seek, to celebrate,
   to embrace that clear
   Tuscany light that
   soothes my spirit.

Sitting in the Church of Sant'
   Agostino, the lovely
   clear winter light
   has sent an almost blinding
   brightness to bathe the interior
   walls so brilliantly
   the 12th century Gozzoli
   frescoes look
   as if they were freshly
   painted yesterday.

Kelly Lombardi

Writing it Down

I sat down to write a short story
about death. It was an autobiography,
and I kept writing it for so long
it wasn't short anymore, and it wasn't
even a story. This was a big problem!

So then, it occurred to me that
no one had ever written a 900 page
autobiographical epic poetic tragedy,
at least none that I had ever seen
or read, so I set about re-writing

the whole ludicrous novella in rhyming
heroic couplets. This was going to take
years, with so few active verbs that
rhyme with New Hampshire, divorce,
and methamphetamine. And I'm always

surrounded by distraction. My thesaurus
is dog-eared and broken-spined with trying
to tell me what all of this history means.
And the history keeps happening; I can't
write it down fast enough!

I don't want anyone to read this work in progress,
but I want everyone to know I'm working on it.
It's self-titled. It will be available only at
independent bookstores, or on 12-inch vinyl.
Millions of readers worldwide will ignore it.

Even the critics will fail to notice.
This would be a complete waste of time,
except that it's built my vocabulary,
and I don't know how to summon
the strength to stop its inertial roll.

My next book, I swear it, will be self-help.
A moneymaker. **Letting Go & Just Gathering Moss**.
I'll know how it ends *before* I start writing it.
I've already written the conclusion.
It will end with "So there!"

Jay Davis

Lizards

Small stripy lizards with
tiny paddy feet are walking
all over and across every
single thought and idea
that goes through my head.

They're not agitated, nor
especially curious, they're just
there, parthenogenesis brings them
to mind I guess. Like some
Escher drawing, but inside.

They're some odd Tourette's syndrome
that only I can hear. But silent.
And reptilian. And tangible, with tails.
Go ahead and say something—
they'll be all over your words like…

well, like lizards, maybe on the outside
of a house down south. I have to
keep carefully shaking them off
just to hear you. That's where
my eyes go sometimes when we talk.

It's why my voice occasionally sounds wrong—
too high, or low, or agitated
when there's nothing to be excited about.
Except these lizards
which I don't want to hurt,

but which distract me. They climb
the screen door between where
your words meet my thoughts.
They let me know
there's a screen there.

Jay Davis

Starfish

The starfish whiskers over the bottom
of the bay on thousands of tiny feet
until it finds a clam or a mussel
of a certain size and positioned so as

to allow it to grasp and then to wrap
its arms around its object of desire,
whence it commences to hug in such a way
as to pull at the halves of the shell.

The pull exerted is gentle at first,
and the nonplussed clam shrugs
its shoulders and purses its lips
and pulls itself snug into its shell.

The starfish is not in a hurry, however,
and those thousands of feet each have tiny suckers
that grasp the surface of the shell so tight
to pull and pull; slowly, ever so slowly.

The hapless mollusk is breathless
from the long embrace,
knows it must open a little
to send a signal to stop,

to let the starfish know it's only a clam
and not the proper object
of such an embrace and so
opens the shell a little

but only the width
of a thin feather of surrender,
and in this gesture the shell is released
just enough for the poised starfish

to exgurgitate its entire stomach
through the very narrow opening
and under this slippery pink blanket
to begin digesting the animal inside.

Jay Davis

A Poem I'll Read On Our First Honest-to-Goodness Date

There are more ways to fail than to succeed.
Sometimes one can become the other.
I'm storing up failures like gunpowder
in the basement. They could come in handy.
I don't know if this pain I'm feeling is the beginning
of a heart attack or acute nicotine withdrawal as I
briskly step outside into the clear air, for a smoke.
What becomes of utility bills 30 days after shut-off?
Or last year's quarterly estimate of income
that was in good faith esteemed as nothing?
If I don't have custody of the kids, then why
do I have custody of their laundry?

All this irony is not lost on me, with a cellar
about to blow. I doubt this poem will get me laid.
I love that you light my cigarettes, but please
be careful not to toss the matches on the floor.
As the picture starts to light up it gets
more upsetting. Damn focus! Damn matches!
And once more I'm going to have to shovel
to clear out the cellar. I have to use this special
plastic trowel. It takes weeks because it's so small,
but I can't risk making sparks. I hope
you're still here when I finish.

Jay Davis

Waving the No-Stick

I'm holding the no-stick in both hands,
swinging it around and back, swatting
with it, like a bat. My arms extend
and my back arches as I swing around
three hundred and sixty degrees, saying
breathlessly, "No, no, and no… no!"
"*Non, jamais*" I say, thinking I'm not
being clear. It's impossible to assent without irony. I hear no assent.

The no-stick is the branch of a tree,
its furthest extent is twigs and leaves,
and its handle is the trunk of the branch
of the tree it was torn from. I'm sweeping
with it through the air, holding the rough,
splintered, torn part in my hands as tight
as I can. My palms are scratched & bleeding,
but my grip holds. This god-forsaken broom says it all for me, "No!"

There's a villain in this story, but the villain
is nowhere near. The no-stick sweeps the area
clear. There's villain, and a hero, and this brilliant
statement I wish were even more eloquent … *No!*

Jay Davis

Reflection on Approaching Fifty

I've tried that "one step to shiny tires,"
gone on to "two steps to a whiter smile,"
and checked into "three steps to a better salary."
I've sequenced all the way to 12-steps
to stop drinking, torturing the children
and feeling so goddamned blue and yet...
and yet, it's still there, the presumption
that there is still something, some
imperfection that I just haven't stepped
up to confront. I've been promised relief
for whatever I suffer from. There are even
products that can relieve the side-effects
of the products that brought the original relief.
Hmmm... someone's making money at this.
Last year the biggest selling medicine was
that drug that lets you have a pet you're
allergic to. You just pay 400 bucks a month
for that bad choice to a pharmaceutical company.
And every product's marketing plan includes
the veiled threat of misery from having dull
dishes, abrasive bathroom tissue, and an
automobile without the built-in excitement
that only a car built with the American know-how
to satisfy a real driving enthusiast can ever rationally fulfill.
We're challenged to not cop to our imperfections
but to hold them back, build a wall, buy a defense.
And yet, and yet... and yet I watched the enthusiasm
of my teens dissipate into the beauty of my twenties.
And the beauty of my twenties was replaced by the
strength of my thirties. And all that power was replaced
in its turn by the blessed mental acuity of my forties.
I'm thinking in my fifties, what will come—it's a cinch
that acuity won't stay—is a lack of illusion. What I see
now is that my kids know my flaws, and friends and
lovers know the same, and I'm trying to surround myself
with friends and acquaintances who aren't fooled either.

Jay Davis

And God knows I've figured out after all these years
how to look at myself in the mirror, and not be fooled
by the clean collar and the deodorant soap, to face it that I'm
less than perfect. Now how do I love that man there?
I'm giving up on self-improvement. Just for today,
I'm only taking that one tiny last step,
to self-acceptance.

Jay Davis

How to Know Everything

Concentrate only on the nonintuitive,
there's no reason to learn the rest.

Assume the lowest motives on the part
of others, and the highest of yourself.

You will often be wrong in this, but
rarely disappointed.

It usually takes less time to find out
you're wrong than that you're right.

You'll never learn why she loves you
and only possibly that she does.

Miracles change everything.
Randomness is unlikely.

The interesting is retained longer though
it is also more likely to be misinterpreted.

You will always know why she doesn't love you,
but rarely that she doesn't, and never when she doesn't.

Having knowledge does not preclude
not acting on it, in fact invites it.

History deceives consistently and retroactively.
Knowledge is safer to pursue in the present.

Fear changes the truth,
no other fact is this scary.

Jay Davis

Shorts

Stirrings
I wake up with my mind full of you
and my hand full of myself.

Eating Disorder
I've been eating lies for so long,
I sometimes think they're nourishing,
have even served them to my guests.

Reconsideration
I'm ready to rethink my misspent youth,
so I'm giving it another chance...

Geography
My home, though I don't necessarily like
the locality, is preferable
to living in the Gray area.

Metamorphosis
Most of the caterpillars
who talk about metamorphosis
haven't emerged yet.

Hurricane Season
I heard the good news this morning
on the radio, that Jerry has been down-
graded to a depression, thank God!

Thief's Generosity
I've stolen nothing
I wouldn't give to you
in a heartbeat

Vow
I solemnly swear, for better or worse,
in sickness and in health, until death do us part,
this divorce shall endure...

Jay Davis

The Human Cannonball

This barrel batters the lately less-willing flesh,
and muzzle speed is becoming an issue.
"A bigger load!" shouts the star to his assistant, who
mutters and obediently increments up the charge.

This enthusiasm to please begins to resemble
self-destruction. A pile of powder this large,
the assistant knows, flirts with immolation. Every show
brings a louder report. Every night another crowd

takes home the memory in ringing ears and wonders
how the Human Cannonball might have done it.
And the stoic assistant shakes his head and wrings his hands
and knows he's already using too much explosive,

that disaster lurks here with this bang and flash and flight.
The Human Cannonball, though, just keeps measuring and
figuring. Traces arcs and trajectories on scraps. It's all
about the numbers now, he wants only the whump and flight of it.

Flying into the face of time—until the net, until the end
of the curve stops him. As the shots get bigger he flies
over further. Flies out, flies into that time that is no time,
that's just ballistics. His assistant mutters and the crowd roars.

Jay Davis

Proposal For A New Artistic Movement

I've finally devised a theory for a life
and artistic movement merged into what
will, one day, be world famous and known as "AI,"
or *"Aggressive Inconsequence."*

Before, why one morning it took me
more than half an hour to remember,
oh yeah! I'm happy! I had to stop
listening to the bad weather channel.

I was experiencing road rage all alone,
in my driveway. And though I'm still
drinking my coffee "on the dark side"
I sweeten it, and lighten it. With half.
And half.

Many people are reluctant to embrace *Aggressive
Inconsequentiality*. It takes courage. It's like
Don Quixote, but without the safety of being fictional,
or the benefit of being Spanish, or a classic.

But I want everyone to be *Aggressively Inconsequential*.
It's our reaction! How else can we counter this other movement,
the one I'm calling *"The New Honesty"*? And what is
the new honesty? Here are some examples:

A boob job? Yes, but—a boob job bought
as a gift by a boyfriend, that makes everyone live
happily ever after. Because now she knows
he loves her. And he does, now.

The New Honesty is a product, like spring water,
or some detergents, that costs less
than its package, and which therefore has
a higher unit price the larger the quantity you buy.

The New Honesty is an auto lease that runs out
after the automobile stops running. And you still

Jay Davis

have to turn it in. It's beef cattle infected from eating the
by-products of beef cattle infected from eating the
by-products of beef cattle infected from eating the
by-products of...

We'll fight all that, my followers and I,
with the bellicose and austere comfort
of AI!! Aggressive Inconsequence says
"I'm mad as hell and I know

I can't do anything about it."
Aggressive Inconsequence says
"I know the fine print is making a lie of the
large print, but I can't read the fine print."

Aggressive Inconsequence says I know
there's no reason for anyone to get up
in the morning but I'm getting out of bed
so maybe I can make breakfast for the rest.

So follow me. Please? Get mad.
Take a plate. Sit down.

Jay Davis

First Snowy Morning

I walked to work this morning,
three or four blocks down Congress Street,
losing about seventy percent of
my body heat right up through my head.
I was emanating it right through my hair
because I'd neglected to wear
my hat. And I'll tell you, it was obvious.
Several people peered at my bare head,
the little aura of steam I exhaled, and
the pink knuckles because of course
I'd left my gloves behind as well.
It's winter now, or very soon.
I have to remember, plan,
and make accommodations for,
even dress for the day that's already outside.
No more spontaneity, not when it's wet
and cold and the world makes the knuckles
achy and stiff. The door's closing
again, for awhile, on the world that feels
like a home, like I can actually live there.
I've got to keep the car warmed up,
myself warmed up even. Wear a coat
and a hat and gloves and good shoes
because the heat is rushing out of the top
of my head like an angel's halo
and it's not warming up the sky one iota.

Jay Davis

Dive Bar

(with a line stolen nearly verbatim from James Tate)

I always try and order the specials when I come out drinking here at
Hope's Saloon. This proprietor spends a lot of time coming up with
new concoctions to keep her menu fresh and interesting, her customers
intrigued. I always order something different, whatever is posted on
the specials board, thinking maybe this time everything will be different.
Hope is always ebullient and has some new plan she's working on— a
tuck or a boob job or this great new facial, new hairstyle, stylish outfit,
amazing new diet, boots that are both warm and sexy. I have two *Satin
Slippers* one night, another time a couple of *Chocolate Martini*'s, a *Blueberry
Margarita*, or that damned beer from China that tastes just like Heineken
but leaves a hangover that lasts as long as the Great Wall. After a few
drinks, though, this place always starts looking just the same. The crowd
thins; Hope slows down too. Of course she's in it for the money, and
no, she's not going home with me even if I wait until her shift is over,
and well… there's always tomorrow, when another drink will be posted
on Hope's chalkboard. The liquor inspector's been in twice in the last
three months. The distributor is starting to leave some items off the
order. We can't smoke in here any more. And Hope is right over there,
stirring things up, rattling some new concoction in her shaker. Who
can argue with Hope? I once said I wouldn't be caught dead in here.
Now I just don't know.

Jay Davis

The Roads in February

In Maine, the roads this time of year
are tossed and lifted and dropped
by the cycle of hard freeze followed
by thaw that's no less hard.

And so with potholes and heaves and jolts the road
I'm driving on seems to chatter and squirm
and shift away from under the wheels,
taking away my direction with it

as if direction were a choice I take lightly.
When there's danger just driving to the store
on an impulse for gas or beer or chocolate,
then choices need to be made carefully.

Last month it occurred to me I no longer aspire
to be happy and passionate and gay so much
as resolute and productive, follow a predictable plan,
and the roads crumble, the wheels go thump.

Jay Davis

Spiritual Bootcamp: the Home Version

Oh certainly, inner peace
could easily be attained
give me thirty days and thirty nights
in some hilltop monastery
simple meals, no talking
wear a saffron robe, you betcha
I'd be serene too.

Those guys have it easy, just coasting really,
not that they haven't earned it, (probably
in their last life as pyramid-building slaves
or scurvy-wracked pilgrims) but the rest of us
down here changing diapers, working
two jobs and having to pay Paul
with what we snatched from Peter,
don't think we are any less holy.
Do not doubt that heavenly armies might have
their own boot camps and that they might
look like exactly like this.

Listen, I've seen the National Geo specials
I've seen the supplicants flay their own hides
for lack of tangible suffering.
Look what I'll endure for You, they are saying,
but I say *Save your hides, Boys.*
Come on over to my house.
Here's where I keep the vacuum.
Here's the number for the sitter — good luck
getting through. Oh, and here's the nice fat stack
of bills. Now come on over here
and let me pin up that robe.
We wouldn't want you tripping
on your way down to the laundry.

Annie Farnsworth

A Good Reason to Retire "The Finger"

I am late for an appointment
and an old man in a Buick
pulls out in front of me, in a big fat hurry
to go 25 in a 40.

I wonder briefly, and with great scorn
if he can actually see where he's going
since the top of his porkpie hat
barely clears the arc of the steering wheel.

A few minutes later
we pass by the scene of an accident -
a tree with its bark shorn,
sun glinting off the raw xylem & phloem,
metal of two cars mingling obscenely
on the sidewalk, burnt smell of hair
and antifreeze searing into my nostrils.

After we've been waved past
I try go back to my Home State of Annoyance
but Mr. Porkpie is nowhere to be seen.
Vanished. Buick and all
and now if you should happen to cut me off
or hold me up in traffic I just say thank you
for whatever you might have just
saved me from.

Annie Farnsworth

The preceding poem was actually a banter poem, which used to be the introduction to the following poem which was inspired by my theory that hosts of angels live among us, many of which are here with no other assignment than just keeping us from killing ourselves out of sheer stupidity. And what a crappy job, really, the traffic angels, in particular, have. This one is a lament, from the point of view of one of them, the one I like to call Our Sister of the Heavenly Tailgate.

The Angel of the Heavenly Tailgate Laments

A few seconds earlier
and you'd have been in front, not behind me.
A few seconds earlier
and you'd still be driving way too fast,
and the little boy's ball would still
be rolling toward the street
there'd still be that slick
of slushy ice at the roadside
left after the last storm.
A few seconds earlier and that dog
would still have chased the squirrel
across the street, you'd have leaned over
to change the radio station, or light
your cigarette, or maybe you dropped
your toll money, or that Coke can
rolled under your brake pedal and what would
have happened then?
Well, you'll never know, so just go ahead
and tailgate, I'm gonna turn off now,
just up ahead here now that the danger's past
and odds are ten-to-one you'll give me the finger
as you go by but I've done my job
and I guess I can't expect you to appreciate
the timing that went into this one.

Annie Farnsworth

Note from a Lost Girl

*(Due to China's one-child rule and the culture's
overwhelming preference for boys, by 1996 there
were 36 million more males in China than females.
The disproportion grows greater each year.)*

What will you do, my brothers,
now that all the sisters have flown,
like little sparrows
across the ocean?
For so many years we've been given away
so they could try again, for you.
Your arrival brought honor
to the family shamed by my birth,
my stay in the orphanage paid
for the clothes on your back,
and you've grown strong
on the milk of my absence.
But what will you do, my brothers,
when you are grown,
and your arms are empty? Will you walk
alone in your old age, with no wife
to steam your rice, or fold your clothes?
Will we seem more precious then?
And what if you came to claim us?
Come, my brothers, to the land
of two-car garages, two-career families
and secondary infertility
where we were welcomed, cherished,
the way you were back home.
It will not be hard to find a lost daughter —
we are many. But do not expect to find us
with eyes cast down, feet bound.
Unabashed I will meet you,
and I will see myself
in the mirror of your face
but your words will fall to the ground
like mistaken sparrows
flown into a pane. You may just ask
for my hand in marriage, I may just ask
if you would like fries with that.

Annie Farnsworth

Feng Shui While Waiting

(for Fu Qian Nuo)

I am trying to keep things simple.
I am trying to clear the clutter
so that when a true thing - like Love –
comes knocking it won't have to compete
with fourteen pairs of shoes,
cartons of outgrown toys and
bank statements from twenty years ago.
When Truth and Beauty arrive
at my front door, the dog should not bark
and frighten them away, nor should Purity
and Innocence have to trip over sleds,
bags of birdseed, and three weeks' worth
of recyclables.

Harboring old building materials
in the subconscious of the basement
is not recommended. One must repair
any plumbing leaks to prevent
good fortune from flowing away,
and one must keep the attic of the mind
in neat and tidy order.
It doesn't hurt to have goldfish, swimming
happily in the wealth corner, as invitation
to prosperity.

But it is not easy, this orderly life,
this paring down to the essential. Are we not trying
to harness same force of creation
that brought us hundreds of thousands
of fish in the sea? butterflies of a million designs?
can we really expect to shape this awesome wind
with tupperware and over-the-door shoe organizers?

You must create a vacuum, the ancient wisdom
instructs, in order for Nature to fill it.
So I'm taking no chances, I've cleaned out
the junk drawer. I've rolled up the rugs

Annie Farnsworth

and scrubbed the rooms of my heart clean.
And I've hung the windchimes
in the doorway, my little one,
so I'll hear you the moment
you breeze in.

Annie Farnsworth

Wading for Poems
(for Martin)

I thought I could just go out and find
a poem. They have not been leaping, lately,
onto the page the way they are wont to
or I want them to, the way the fat
and disintegrating salmon crowd
each other out of the very creeks
they're trying to swim up to spawn.
I've never been one to sit at my desk,
expecting words to join me at certain times
as in a support group or canasta club,
for me it's more like yardwork, raking words
into piles, or planting seeds and then coming back
to walk the rows with a basket, picking
the ripened premise.

So I go down back of the house
where I know spring has flooded
beneath the birches a fleeting swamp.
I've got my rubber boots on
and stand in the middle, thinking surely
the poem will meet me there.
While I'm waiting I fall up, or is it down,
through the graphite branches into the sky
into another whole place and still, the poem's
a no-show. Silly woman, I think later, while
propping my boots to dry, a real poem does not try
to wade out to meet itself. But then,
who says I have to write
that kind?

Annie Farnsworth

This Poem and I Need a Room

I am walking back from the mailbox
and black and orange beetles, looking for other
beetles with the requisite DNA,
are drunkenly flinging themselves into my hair
and the tops of my feet are dusted gold
with what the aspens and birches
have shamelessly flung out to the wind.
Oh sure, they seem demure, their limbs
and torsos poised just so, but look again:
the dance of their sex is in the air.
Even the sparrows have forgotten
their graceful reputations, flapping and falling
off branches in their awkward fumbling
through each other's hindfeathers.

I don't know what I can reveal
about spring, and sex, that some other poet
hasn't already penned in the past
two thousand years. But we never
tire of it, do we? Oh, we have our distractions:
there are whole industries of garden fountains
and barbecue grills, there are monogrammed
croquet sets, and gold-plated tools for turning
the soil without touching it. There's even a
Perennial-of-the-Month Club, which saves your soul
from the temptations awaiting one brazen enough
to step into the steamy salesroom of the greenhouse.
Forget that whole cable channel of garden shows
that enables the armchair voyeur to watch
someone ELSE fondling the painted ferns,
or pruning the Japanese maple.
Forget the promises inherent in twelve chemical steps
to a greener lawn — I mean, who are we kidding?
How far can we get from the titillating truth,
which is that right now, every living thing out there
is vibrating at the speed of love.

Annie Farnsworth

Just take off your hat and your shoes.
Just walk out to your mailbox, or anywhere,
for that matter, and let the universe
make love to you
with every
slow step
you take.

Annie Farnsworth

Spaghetti Western Days

(for Jacob)

My son, just turned five
has not learned the rules about wild versus tame.
Always busy, transplanting field violets
and dandelions into my garden to make it
"more beautiful," smuggling toads
and millipedes into the house to keep for pets.
I mourn those small lives whose tiny,
dessicated remains I must chip from the windowsills,
shake from shoeboxes, and I try to explain
why we must leave nature where it is.

But this is a boy who snitches
my scotch tape and writing paper
to roll his own "cigarettes," who knows
that the good guys wear white hats
but he wants a black one anyway. A boy
with holsters and spurs, no horse in sight.
Days like this, when both front and back doors
flap like wings, and the big pine out back
flies a banner of kite tail,
I see that my doorstep is no boundary
and that there are frontiers I haven't yet
got eyes to see. And if I know anything,
just one damn thing worth knowing
in this lifetime I've learned it only since
this whirlwind of a boy
blew into town.

Annie Farnsworth

Casting

Yes, there was Light,
in the beginning and Oh how quickly
we came to underrate it
           forgetting
how entire worlds, like the moon,
just for example,
can be pared down to nothing
but the white of a nearly-closed eye —
           for no more
compelling reason than our
stumbling, blindly,
into its way.
           So often we cast
shadows as the lead
characters — the baby who was born
so still; the woman wronged, a father
gone mad —
           or stage a shadowy set:
the empty fairgrounds, blown
by a littered breeze, the desolation
of the parking lot where we've forgotten
where we've parked
        and that's another thing; how we
can't even make it to the theatre on time
how our memories leave us, as do our keys,
our sense of direction
        so when we show up
the theatre is already darkened
and we stumble down the aisle
to the only empty seat, behind some
voluminous head of hair or in front of
a child who will kick our ass
from previews to credits
        so consider, if you must,
the lilies of the fields but do take note
of which way their newly minted
and glinting faces are turned;

Annie Farnsworth

not up at the stage where the dreaded
Scarpia will doubtless enter,
Violetta will surely gag out her last,
          but back toward the booth
whence all the pretty pictures come, whence
all the pure and flittering light streams
the projectionist always faceless
and aiming just over
our heads

Annie Farnsworth

Banter Poem

I was doing just fine at this sort of thing
Read a poem, do a little banter, read another one –
Until at one reading some guy yelled out
(not to me but to some other poor bum
though it could just as easily have been me),
but anyway he yelled out
cut the chit-chat, just read the damned poem
which seemed incredibly rude
but I asked around and come to find out
the protocols for proper reading have shifted and
now, it is terribly gauche to banter
in between poems. You're supposed to just read
the poem, stop, read the next poem, and if
you feel compelled to explain or provide anecdotes
for any of them it's just proof that the poem
itself was painfully inadequate and I sure
can't have that so I took all that stuff
I usually say in between the poems, wrote it
down and made it into poems figuring
what the hell no one'll be the wiser
and that worked for a while and then I felt
compelled to explain why every other poem
sounded like banter while the ones in between
sounded like normal poems, but that too
was banter so I then had to write this
poem. And if I ever see that guy at another
poetry reading I don't know whether to thank him
for my new obsessive compulsive disorder and
ask him to split the cost of the meds
or if I should just thank him
for all the new poems.

Annie Farnsworth

Buddha's Mother Had Her Worries Too

If they'd had them back then, I'll bet
Buddha's mother would have smoked Pall Malls.
And if there'd been cable, I can see her
watching Montel, or Sally Jesse Raphael,
wondering, nervously, if anyone else
has her problem.
Why can't he be like the other kids,
she thinks, taking a big drag,
What am I doing wrong?

He doesn't play
like the other kids, always
twirling flowers by their stems
smiling beatifically at nothing much
all the neighbors think
he's retarded.
And certainly I'm biased, she thinks,
but there's something special
about him, just give him
some time.

Annie Farnsworth

Love's Aroma

I've pondered what you mean
when you say you are in it
for the long haul.
You will love me forever, you will be there
when I need you. If I got cancer, you once told me,
you would not mind my head
bald from chemo. You would love me fat or thin,
or singing off-key. You'd love me blonde,
brunette, or redhead, you'd love me
without legs. *We'd just get you one of those*
powered jobbies, you say, *and put a ramp out front.*
You say you will be there
for the long haul, and I'm sure
your intentions are good
but you forgot to mention the disclaimer
to your definition of "always"
which I've just recently discovered really means
"as long as I don't have to wash
the shit off the dog." I don't care what anyone says
about unconditional love. It is not
a river, a rose, a song we never tire
of hearing. Let's face it, Love is more
like camouflage, and the long haul is littered
with carcasses. Our success may well be contingent
upon a poor sense of smell, an appreciation
of what we each had to roll through
just to get here.

Annie Farnsworth

THE POETS

Eva Miodownik Oppenheim has lived in New York City since her arrival as a refugee child from Nazi Germany during World War II, after a two year stopover in Montevideo, Uruguay. A graduate of Queens College, CUNY, she also studied in Stratford-upon-Avon, England, and in the Writing Division of Columbia University's School of the Arts. Her first career was as an actress, under the name Eva Mio, in summer stock and Off-Broadway. She went on to write publicity for films in London and books in New York, working also as a freelance editor. Most recently, she served as a senior administrator in alumnae affairs at Barnard College, Columbia U. Oppenheim's poems have appeared in *Animus, Off the Coast, Poetica, The Little Magazine, Kolenu,* Third Annual *Live Poets Society Anthology,* and two volumes of *New Voices: American Writing Today,* the *Comstock Review* and *Jewish Women's Literary Annual.* She has given readings at the Harlow Art Gallery in Hallowell, Maine, on WBAI (NYC) and at public and private venues in New York City.

Patrick Hicks teaches creative writing at Augustana College and was recently a Visiting Fellow at Oxford. His work has appeared in over fifty publications, and he has enjoyed long residences in England, Northern Ireland, Germany, and Spain. He was a finalist for the *New Letters* Literary Award and he won the Weseca Arts Council Poetry Prize. He currently lives in Sioux Falls, South Dakota, where he enjoys thunderstorms rolling across the prairie.

Dennis Camire currently divides his time between teaching part-time at Southern Maine Community College, bartending at various restaurants in Southern Maine, and fulfilling his duties as courier/Associate Editor of Sheltering Pines Press. Some of his poems have appeared in *Poetry East, The Mid-American Review, Off the Coast, The Taj Mahal Review, Words and Images, A Sense of Place: Collected Maine Poems,* and on a variety of spoken word CDs. *Unidentified Flying Odes* is his second chapbook; his first was *Bio-Luminescing,* published by Sheltering Pines Press.

Dr. Blaine McCormick is the Associate Dean for Undergraduate Programs at the Hankamer School of Business at Baylor University. He holds an appointment on the management faculty and teaches negotiation and conflict resolution at the undergraduate, graduate, and executive levels. He was honored to receive the 2002-03 Collins Outstanding Professor Award granted each spring by the graduating senior class. Dr. McCormick has published a variety of books, scholarly articles, and poems. A nationally recognized scholar on the business practices of Benjamin Franklin and Thomas

Edison, Dr. McCormick is interviewed frequently in the media, including the *New York Times, CNN*, and *ABC World News Tonight with Peter Jennings*. Dr. McCormick serves as an editor for Volume Six of *The Papers of Thomas A. Edison*. Before joining the Baylor faculty, Dr. McCormick worked in Dallas and Plano for ARCO Oil & Gas Company as a human resource management professional and held a faculty appointment at Pepperdine University in Malibu, California. He lives in Waco with his wife of 16 years, Sarah, and their three children – Ellis, Miriam, and Bea.

Marita O'Neill teaches eleventh grade English at Scarborough High School. She lives in Portland, Maine with her partner Duff; they sometimes venture as far south as Boston to catch a Celtics game for fun. She has an M.F.A. in poetry from Vermont College. Her first chapbook was called *Love Dogs*. Email her at moneill1212@maine.rr.com.

Kevin Sweeney has been teaching English at Southern Maine Community College for over twenty years. He holds degrees from California (PA) State College and the University of Massachusetts. His work has appeared in a number of lit-mags, and he has twice been nominated for a Pushcart Prize. He lives in South Portland, Maine, with wife and pets. He hopes to one day be an old gringo in Mexico watching Pittsburgh Steelers games via satellite. He has been on a diet, with lapses, for forty-six years.

Don Moyer was born in Brooklyn, NY. The family moved to the South Bronx in the late 1940's. His father, Howard, and mother, Sally, operated a candy store near the old Third Avenue Elevated Railway. The family moved to rural, upstate New York when he was seven. Don still lives in upstate New York, near Saratoga Springs. As a young man, Don hitchhiked across the country, rode Southern Pacific freights through the Southwest desert, and finally graduated from Westfield (Massachusetts) College in 1972. He has been employed as a factory worker at Strathmore Paper and the Columbia Bicycle Company in Massachusetts, and as a high school teacher, in both public and private, city and rural schools. Eighteen years ago, Don started a one-person interior landscaping business. He has been married to his wife, Susan, for twenty-seven years. They have a seventeen year-old daughter, Kate, and a twenty two year-old son, Nick. Don's poetry has appeared in *Poetry, Harpers, Antaeus, Rolling Stone,* and *The Massachusetts Review*, among other publications. His previous book of poetry, WHEN, was published in 2003 by Bottom Dog Press.

Tom A. (TA) Delmore is a published poet living in Mill Creek, Washington. He has been married for twenty-seven years and has two grown children. He is currently a shuttle bus driver for Microsoft, which gives him more time to write.

Michelle Lewis' poetry and critical essays have appeared in *Café Review*, *Kalliope*, *Chester H. Jones Anthology*, *Food for Thought*, *Poet Lore* and *The Gettysburg Review*. She lives in Cape Elizabeth, Maine.

M. Kelly Lombardi is a practicing and teaching poet who lives in coastal Washington County in a book-filled music- laden house with her faithful dog, Lucca. Her credits include Wolf Moon Journal, MVNO, Better Homes and Gardens, Aroostook Review, Coastal Courier, Narramissic Journal, Stanza and Christian Science Monitor, among others. She teaches poetry in the Sunrise Seniors College at the local university, specializing in contemporary Irish poets, international poets and how-to-write-poetry. She also lectures on antique roses and raises about 50 varieties of same. She goes to Ireland each year to refresh on Irish music and sit in on poetry readings, as well as going to Italy where she stays at a 12th century Augustinian monastery and writes, writes, writes. Ireland is her ancestral home, Italy is her spiritual home, and Maine is her home port.

Jay Davis was born and raised in NH, and now lives and works in Portland, ME. He has previously published poetry in *The Café Review* and *Monkey's Fist*, and criticism in *Animus*. The volume you are holding, *The Hard Way*, is his second chapbook with Moon Pie Press. *The Hard Way* is his second chapbook; the first was *Whispers, Cries and Tantrums*, published in 2005 by Moon Pie Press.

Annie Farnsworth is a poet, a mom, a Reiki Master, artist, gardener, and lives in southern Maine with her two kids and a variety of furry critters. She has a B.A. in English with a minor in art history from USM, and because one unmarketable, esoteric degree did not seem like enough, she went on to receive her Master of Science in Metaphysics. She is now working to add other letters to her name like PhD, RN, and LOL. When she is not editing, studying, making stuff, and floor sweeping, Annie works as a psych. tech in an acute-care mental health facility. Sometimes she is unreasonably happy just to sit on the porch with a cuppa and listen to the crickets.